New England Wild Places

Michael Tougias

Covered Bridge Press
North Attleborough, Massachusetts

To Helen and Stanley

ISBN 0-924771-88-7

Covered Bridge Press
7 Adamsdale Road
North Attleborough, MA 02760
(508) 761-7721

10 9 8 7 6 5 4 3 2 1

Contents

Acknowledgements

My pleasure in discovering the wild places would not be possible without the efforts of many unheralded people giving their time to protect New England's open spaces, and I thank them on behalf of all the hikers, canoeists and outdoor lovers who cherish the woods and water. As I wrote each chapter, I often thought that if not for a few individuals, the places I've come to love might be lost forever. I also thought of the companionship of friends who made the trips special, and for my wife Mary Ellen's understanding while I was researching and writing. Finally, I'd like to thank Chuck Durang, my publisher, for believing in this project, as well as in my novel *Until I Have No Country*.

Michael J. Tougias

Author's Note

"It's the exploration and discovery that gives you a high—it's the closest thing to being a child again," answered my brother Mark. I had just explained to him the feeling of joy that came over me during one of my solo outings.

He was right of course, and the "high" he was talking about can be a powerful thing, maybe too powerful. It causes me continually to go off, usually alone, to places that others bypass. Once you have that special feeling, you want it again, and so you search.

But there are worse addictions to have, and if you are going to be a modern-day explorer, New England has the diversity to make each outing different from the last. My selections are special places where solitude is still possible, where energy is felt, and where spirits linger. Best of all, I've only scratched the surface of all the wild places to be explored, and many more await discovery.

Michael J. Tougias

New England
Wild Places

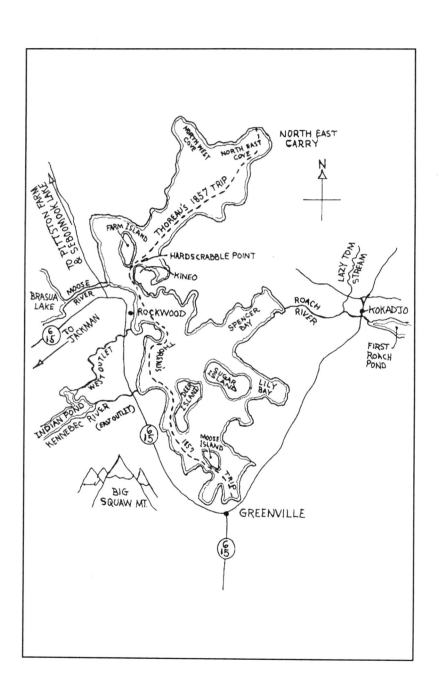

Moosehead Lake, Mount Kineo and the Kennebec River

"Make sure you tell someone you're paddling to Kineo," said a friend who grew up on Moosehead Lake.

"Why?" I asked.

"So they'll know where to drag the lake."

It was my friend's way of warning me about the waves in the narrow passage between Rockwood and Mount Kineo. He told me he thought my plans for paddling solo through it in my twelve-foot canoe were crazy, adding that it wasn't uncommon for the waves to kick up to four- and five-foot swells.

I'd done enough hair-brained things in my trips around New England to know that, if I were a cat, I'd have used up most of my nine lives, so when I arrived at Moosehead later that summer I first tried a paddle in a more sheltered area at Lily Bay.

No sooner did I leave the cove at the boat launch than I began a running battle with the wind, which seemed determined to keep me from crossing Lily Bay over to Sugar Island. The wind won, and I elected to hug the shore, heading in a southerly direction.

Bleached driftwood, pointed fir and stunted cedars cover the boulder-strewn shoreline, and I realized why people have a fascination with Maine's largest lake. Five hundred islands dot

1

the surface, and much of its 400 miles of shore is undeveloped—the cry of loon is more likely to be heard than the roar of a jet ski.

I paddled for a couple hours, and although I saw a number of loons and several great blue heron, what's a trip to Moosehead Lake without seeing a moose? So I returned to the car, and drove northward up the eastern side of the lake toward Kakadjo, where the blacktop ends and the gravel roads of the paper companies begin.

Just north of Kakadjo a broad marsh surrounds Lazy Tom stream, and it was here that I saw my first moose, feeding at the edge of the stream about 500 yards away. The wind was gusting through the marsh, but I wouldn't have to worry about waves, so I launched my canoe and slowly paddled toward the moose. Looking through the telephoto lens on my camera I could see it was a male with the prongs of new antlers still covered in velvet. Its great head dipped below the water's surface, emerging with a mouthful of aquatic plants.

The eyesight of the moose is not very good, but their hearing and sense of smell are keen, so this young bull knew I was approaching, but didn't seem particularly alarmed. The wind was at my back pushing me directly at the moose, which allowed me to concentrate on photography. Each shot filled more and more of the picture frame with the brown beast. Soon its head filled the entire frame, and when I peered over the top of the camera, I found that I'd drifted to within twenty feet.

I didn't move a muscle, scared of what he might do if I startled him. Although I'd seen moose before, I'd never been this close, never been in a canoe seat looking *up* at one. I could hear him chomping the weeds, imagining I'd get a whiff of his breath next. All the while the wind was pushing me closer.

I figured he would submerge his head again and that would be my chance to back-paddle, but instead his eyes were fixed on me.

Then his nostrils flared, his ears twitched and he emitted a deep, guttural snort, almost a "woof," like an angry dog makes. I almost wet my pants. When something that big—seven feet high at the shoulder and weighing about 1,200 pounds—makes what I perceive to be a threatening noise I pay attention. With heart pounding I fumbled for the paddle and backed off.

From a more comfortable distance of about forty feet I calmed down and watched him resume feeding. Fear of a moose may be laughed at by some, but it's a prudent response when encountering any wild animal not giving ground. While moose are normally docile, they have been known to chase and even attack people. I recall reading of one moose terrorizing a deer hunter, pursuing him for over an hour, as the hunter raced around trees before finally hiding under a pile of logs. Autumn is the season to worry most, when the bulls are in surly moods, looking for mates. And even in the spring, a cow with calves is not to be trifled with.

Henry David Thoreau described moose as "great frightened rabbits, with their long ears and half-inquisitive, half-frightened looks: the true denizens of the forest." He thought the moose a strange and awkward creature, asking, "Why should it stand so high at the shoulders? Why have so long a head? Why have no tail to speak of?"

As I sat in my canoe I agreed that it is one of the oddest-looking creatures I've seen. A bit of tattered fur hung from its chin, and each time it lifted its head from feeding, water would cascade down its large snout. Plants streamed from its mouth as it chomped away, enormous ears aimed in my direction, and small eyes still glaring at me. He clearly had no intention of leaving the spot.

He must have been hungry to have walked a good distance over open marsh to reach the stream in the middle of the day. Normally moose stay in the forest during the day, eating a browse of leaves and twigs (their Algonquian name is "twig eater"), or resting in the shade. In the evening they venture to more open country of clear-cut and marshes to feed throughout the night and into the morning.

Perhaps the moose in front of me was driven from the woods by the black flies that still lingered. The open marsh was relatively free of bugs and he would find complete relief if he submerged himself in the water. I left him to his salad, and paddled back to where I had left my car.

North of Kakadjo, one can access the deepest recesses of the Maine woods, courtesy of the roads cut by the paper companies. The most celebrated of these roads is the Great Northern Paper Company's "Golden Road," a ribbon of gravel running east and west for ninety-six miles through dense forest. The road transverses uninhabited stretches of wilderness from Millonocket to the Canadian border at St. Zacharie, Quebec. When encountering lumber trucks barrelling down the road loaded with timber for the mills, private cars are advised to pull over to the shoulder.

Prior to the Golden Road's completion in 1975, lumbermen moved timber and supplies on simple tote roads that were narrow and winding. The roads would be used while there was activity in the region and then later abandoned, reverting back to forest. The Golden Road was the first of several roads built to last. Thirty feet wide, laid out relatively straight, and open year-round, it cost considerably more to build than the tote roads, and Great Northern accountants dubbed it the Golden Road because it cost $45,000 a mile to construct.

When traveling the paper company roads it's best to come prepared to spend the night in case your car conks out. These are isolated roads, where shutting off the engine usually means total silence. Don't expect to see many other motorists, and forget about service stations. In fact about the only man-made destination which draws people is Pittston Farm, a combination campground, inn and restaurant that has quite a reputation in the north woods. Located northwest of Moosehead Lake near the western end of Seeboomook Lake, Pittston Farm describes its restaurant as "lumber-camp cooking served lumber-camp style." Loggers, hunters, fishermen, and lately the general public have discovered its home-cooked food, served in heaping proportions befitting a lumberjack.

I poked farther north of Kakadjo, looking for brook-trout streams, but dusk was falling so I stopped at Kakadjo (population "not many") to fish the Roach River below the dam at First Roach Pond. The water here is fly-fishing only, catch and release, and I soon found out what a good policy that was. In the fading light I tied on a gaudy streamer and cast into churning white water beneath the dam. The current formed an eddy and my line was carried back toward me rather than away, so I stripped it quickly. As soon as the slack was out a fish hit.

The word "vicious" seems to be an overworked description of a strike, but that's the kind of powerful hit this was, topped off with a catapulting leap and a flash of silver. It was a salmon, about fifteen inches, and it rocketed out of the water like a missile from a submarine. It took me three tries with my net before landing it. Even in the twilight its silvery skin seemed to shine from within, and I admired its sleek shape before slipping it back into the river.

Back in Greenville I checked into the Greenville Inn. Many people are surprised that Moosehead Lake has upscale accommodations, expecting that such a remote region would only offer camping or cabins. The Greenville Inn is about a far from roughing as you can get. It was built in 1895 by a lumber baron, and carpenters labored for ten years to carve the embellishments in the woodwork and the mantels over the many fireplaces, and lay the mosaic and English tiles. Up the stairway and past the large spruce tree painted on a leaded window are seven elegant guestrooms with antique furnishings. One room even has a "needle shower" where the water sprays not only from above but from the sides as well. Beyond the inn and farther up the hillside are handsome cottages, each with a nice view of East Cove Harbor and Squaw Mountain.

The Greenville Inn is family-owned and operated by Michael, Elfi and Susie Schnetzer. Michael oversees the dining room and the upkeep of the inn (he built the cottages), Susie is the pastry chef and gardener, and Elfi is the dinner chef. A restaurant critic wrote that Susie and Elfi have a "flair for perfection," which was evident during my visit from the happy faces I saw seated in a full dining room.

After dinner I curled up with my copy of Thoreau's *Maine Woods,* and although I intended to turn in early I ended up reading until one o'clock in the morning. There is something special about reading the work of a master when the subject matter is right outside your door.

Thoreau explored the Maine woods three times from 1846 to 1857, each time humbled by the wildness of the region's rivers, lakes and mountains. Moosehead Lake figured prominently in his final trip when he and traveling companion Edward Hoar and native American guide Joe Polis set out from Greenville, at the southern end of the lake, and canoed northward. At the top of the lake they portaged over the northeast carry and on into the west branch of the Penobscott River, then through a series of lakes and streams, before finally making their way to the east branch of the Penobscott which would carry them toward Bangor and civilization. Thoreau selected this route over other possibilities because it went through "the wildest country."

A week before the trip, Thoreau turned forty. He knew that travel had the power to recharge both the body and the spirit, and Maine had all the ingredients for the exploration he loved most. He could learn from his native guide, see a side of nature different than Concord, and test his skills in a grueling journey. His stamina and strength are seldom mentioned, but Thoreau was a rugged individual not afraid of hardship. He would think nothing of setting out from Concord for long treks that spanned many days, and in Maine he impressed his guide with his vigor, even beating him a portage race.

Thoreau had a keen sense of humor that shines in his writing of the Maine woods. Even the stagecoach ride from Bangor to Greenville was written in a light vein, as when he discussed a dog on the stage that jumped off and caused a delay while the owner searched for it. "This dog was depended on to stop bears with. He had already stopped one somewhere in New Hampshire, and I can testify that stopped a stage in Maine." He noted that the dog rode on the roof of the stage for free, while he had to pay for the canoe that, unlike the dog, "lay still on the top," being lashed to the stage.

On July 24th at four o'clock in the morning the three men pushed off from Greenville in a birchbark canoe as "closely packed as a market-basket, and might possibly have been upset without spilling any of its contents." He expresses his joy over setting out after the stage ride by writing, "It was inspiring to hear the regular dip of the paddles, as if they were our fins or flippers, and to realize that we were at length fairly embarked. We who had felt strangely as stage-passengers and tavern-lodgers were suddenly naturalized there and presented with the freedom of the lakes and the woods."

During his first night in the woods, he could hardly contain his exuberance, waking Edward Hoar to show him a piece of phosphorescent wood that glowed in the night. "I was exceedingly interested in this phenomenon, and already felt paid for my journey. I let science slide, and rejoiced in that light as if it had been a fellow-creature. A scientific explanation, as it is called, would have been altogether out of place there. That is for pale daylight."

For Thoreau, travel was to be done at a slow pace, preferably under your own power by paddle or foot, and curiosity rather than destination should be your guide.

* * * *

The next morning I set off for Mount Kineo. In the early morning fog the steamer Katahdin loomed like something from a lost era. Built in 1914 at the Bath Iron Works, the Katahdin was one of many boats that cruised the lake bringing supplies to hunting camps and resorts. But with the advent of better roads, all the boats went out of service except the Katahdin, which was relegated to towing booms of logs down the lake until the nation's last log drive in 1975. Saved from the scrap heap by the nonprofit Moosehead Marine Museum, she was refurbished, and again carries passengers from Greenville to Rockwood and Kineo.

Greenville still conjures up the feeling of a frontier town, and I'm reminded of James Russell Lowell's portrayal of it as appearing to have "dripped down from the hills and settled in the hollow at the foot of the lake." It acts as the gateway to the north woods, not only via the logging roads but also by the flying service companies whose float planes are scattered about the shoreline. Folsom's Flying Service, another family-owned enterprise, has been taking sportsmen into the backwoods for over fifty years. And as if to underscore that this is still a frontier, Max Folsom has also had his share of rescue missions, sometimes flying out survivors and victims of boating and hunting accidents.

As I drove through Greenville, past tiny Thoreau Park and the Road Kill Café, I glimpsed the lake, but never saw its magnitude, because of the many points of land that cut off the full north–south view. There is only a hint of its true proportions—40 miles long, covering 100 square miles in area. Equally remarkable is the fact that its inlet (the Moose River) and outlet (the source of the Kennebec) are on the same side, no more than a mile apart.

Rockwood lies about halfway up the west side of the Lake, with Mount Kineo looming across the water to the east, and together they give Moosehead its hour-glass shape, with the passage between them the constricted middle. When I arrived at Rockwood the waves were about two and a half feet, with a stiff breeze blowing from the north; not the kind of waters for canoeing. Even if I made it across to the Kineo peninsula, the weather could take a turn for the worse and I'd be stuck for the night, sleeping under the canoe.

When Thoreau approached Kineo from the south he recorded a near-capsizing and likened the waves at Kineo to monsters, showing his talent for writing dramatic imagery:

"Here we were exposed to the wind from over the whole breadth of the lake and ran a little risk of being swamped. While I had my eye fixed on the spot where a large fish had leaped, we took in a gallon or two of water, which filled my lap … . Again we crossed a broad bay opposite the mouth of the Moose River, before reaching the narrow straight at Mount Kineo, made what the voyageurs call a traverse, and found the water quite rough. A very little wind on these broad lakes raises a sea which will swamp a canoe. Looking off from a lee shore, the surface may appear to be very little agitated, almost smooth, a mile distant, or if you see a few white crests they appear nearly level with the rest of the lake; but when you get out so far, you may find quite a sea running, and erelong, before you think of it, a wave will gently creep up the side of the canoe and fill your lap, like a monster deliberately covering you with its slime before it swallows you, or it will strike the canoe violently, and break into it."

Even the guide remarked several times that he did not like to cross the lakes "in littlum canoe."

And so with the waves breaking loudly before me and Thoreau's warning confirming that of my friend, I left my Old Town Pack canoe on top of the car and waited for the boat that shuttles passengers between Rockwood and Kineo. It's funny how smells and sounds can trigger memories, and as I sprawled in the sun, the sound of the waves took me back to an earlier visit here when I was a boy. My family had rented a ramshackle cabin at the edge of Moosehead and I recall my parents saying they barely slept a wink the first night due to the crashing waves and the howling wind. I slept like a baby, relieved that an earlier incident had not turned into serious trouble.

I'd wandered away from the cabin with my younger brother in tow to go exploring. We followed a trail that first hugged the shoreline and then veered inland along the edge of a small swamp. As we rounded a bend, a moose came trotting up the trail directly at us, and we froze, staring and blinking, never having seen a moose before. For some reason the moose did not turn tail and run, nor did it stop, but kept coming, its gangly legs swallowing up the ground between us. I ran of course, forgetting my younger brother—something he reminds me of to this day.

The arrival of the shuttle broke me out of my reminiscence. It's an open-air pontoon boat capable of holding about a dozen people. Only four of us boarded, me for the mountain and three for the Kineo House, a six-room inn located at the base of the mountain. Through the years various hotels have come and gone on Kineo (most burned), with the most elaborate being the Mount Kineo Hotel, large enough to host 700 guests. Part of the draw of the hotel was the constant breeze which kept away the mosquitoes and black flies, and the altitude which prevented hay fever and asthma. Built in 1884, the resort featured a telegraph, billiard halls, 400-seat dining room, elevators, post office and orchestra performances.

In many respects Kineo and Moosehead are wilder now than at the turn of the century. But if not for recent action by the people of Maine, Mount Kineo could have become a tangle of condominiums or a playground of the rich. In 1987 voters approved a $35 million bond issue to finance a land-acquisition program called Land for Maine's Future. And what a program it was—60,000 acres of scenic countryside were protected from development, including three and one half miles of Kineo lake front. Now anyone with a yen for adventure and eye for beauty can visit Kineo, and see it much as it was when Thoreau was there.

Crossing the three-quarter-mile narrows affords an impressive prospect of Mount Kineo's cliffs rising 800 feet straight up from the lake. Kineo means "sharp peak" in Abenaki, and native American legend says this ancient mountain of rock is a petrified moose killed by Glooskap, a figure from native American mythology (although I didn't see the resemblance, its said that the steep side of the mountain looks like the head of a moose).

But its the composition of Kineo's stone, rhyolite dating back 375 million years, that attracted native Americans here because of the way it fractured to make arrow heads, spear heads, scrapers and other implements. Native Americans from all over New England would make the journey to Kineo to gather this raw material. At the south face of the mountain, rocks would break off from the cliff, shattering at the bottom and forming jagged pieces ready for the tool maker to gather and chip into the desired forms. At various "workshops" below the cliffs and close to the water's edge, native Americans would sort and then work the stone.

The shuttle boat handled the waves with ease, dropping me off at a cove near the Kineo House after a ten-minute ride. Then I walked to the trail head, following a shoreline path, with the lake on one side and woods of white birch, maple, pine and beech on the other. The trail begins about a half mile down the path, curling away from the water to climb the mountain's spine. A plantation of red pine gives way to spruce, fir and oak, while magnificent southern views begin to appear at dizzying heights. Endless green conifers, the sparkling blue waters of Moosehead, and dark islands stretching toward hazy purple mountains all greet the hiker.

Such scenes put a spring in my step and had my spirits soaring. On a hike like this, when you're seeing the world with a fresh eye, the labor of the climb is enjoyable and welcome.

Even the burn in the legs and the shortness of breath make you feel alive, thankful for the two legs that can carry you to such beauty.

Of the hundred's of hikes I've made, I soon voted Kineo my favorite. How can you not love a climb that rises from the middle of a lake?

It takes about an hour and half to reach the summit, where a fire tower offers an even better view than those seen on the walk up. I have a fear of exposed heights, but my desire for a 360-degree vista was stronger, and I inched my way to the top, white-knuckling the steel railing. But once there I was surprisingly at ease—maybe I was swept up by the scenery, taken away to another world for awhile.

If I lived out west, in big-sky country where one can see for miles, Kineo might not have affected me so powerfully. But here in New England, where trees and undulating hills block much of the sky and distant terrain, we come to rely on other senses when in the woods. The little things are noticed, like the scent of ferns, the texture of birchbark, and the song of the wood thrush. In the rare instances when we are afforded a view like the one from Kineo, it seems all the more remarkable, as if true vision had previously been denied us.

I spent quite a while at the top, scanning the horizon. To the north is the upper half of Moosehead, and I could imagine Thoreau, Hoar and Polis, paddling their birchbark canoe to the northeast carry, eager to reach the Penobscott. To the south, Big Squaw Mountain dominates, and to the southwest is the beginning of the Kennebec River, while the western view reveals the end of the Moose River. The work of the glaciers is evident on either side of Kineo, with Blue Ridge Mountain and Little Kineo Mountain shaped similarly to Kineo and in perfect alignment. All have a sheer vertical southeast face and are smooth-sloped on the northwest side. But the most interesting sight I saw was a man-made one, when I looked *down* at a float plane flying by.

Not wanting to end the good feeling at the summit, I climbed off the tower and followed a path to a nearby cliff with a southern overlook. Low bush blueberries were scattered about and I helped myself, then lay down on the ledge and watched the clouds sail by, feeling lucky that simple pleasures are the ones that bring me the most joy. I looked forward to the day when my son could make this climb with me. Mountaintops are sacred places, and I thanked the higher power for creating Kineo, the wind that whistled by, and the sun that warmed my face. Everyone should feel the peace and power of this wild place.

It wasn't until two weeks later when I began organizing my notes that I realized I'd climbed the mountain on the same day of the year as Thoreau, July 24. He also hiked up via the same trail, writing, "The clouds breaking away a little, we had a glorious wild view, as we ascended, of the broad lake with its fluctuating surface and numerous forest-clad islands, extending beyond our sight both north and south ... ." He was awed by the precipice at the summit, remarking, "we looked, and probably might have jumped down to the water, or to the seemingly dwarfish trees on the narrow neck of land which connects it with the main. It is a dangerous place to try the steadiness of your nerves."

I was glad that Thoreau got to experience Kineo before his death just five years later.

Coming off the mountain, I mistakenly took a path that began descending the cliffs in a more direct route where I had to use hands as well as feet to stay on the faint trail. At the base of a ledge, the path petered out and I recognized my error, but I had the good fortune to come upon a pile of stones that looked recently chipped. Thoreau said that the rhyolite becomes "a uniform white where exposed to the light and air." I put one of the sandy white stones with a ragged edge in my pack to bring to my wife's uncle Stanley, an eighty-seven-year-old archaeologist who made a pilgrimage to Kineo to gather rocks some thirty years ago.

Once off the mountain I followed a shoreline path toward Hardscrabble Point at the northwest end of the mountain. But after walking a half mile, the lure of the lake was too much and I undressed and jumped into its cold, clear waters, bobbing on the waves like a loon. If one could climb a mountain and follow it up by a swim on a daily basis I'd wager they would live to a hundred. That's how good it felt.

After the swim I sat on a rock, opened my pack and laid my sandwich next to me. A wave came in, and in my haste to keep my pack from getting wet I forgot about the sandwich, which got soaked. But when you're in the woods and you've just been climbing, appetite is a powerful thing, and I ate the soggy meal. Now I have Moosehead in both body and spirit.

Thoreau, Hoar and Polis camped on this spot their first night of the trip. It was here that Polis asked if Thoreau had ever heard "Indian sing," and Thoreau was touched by the song: "There was indeed a beautiful simplicity about it ... the sentiments of humility and reverence chiefly were expressed." Prior to the song, Thoreau seemed to have his doubts about Polis, writing in his journal that when they were temporarily lost in the mist on the lake he asked Polis the way and he answered, "I don't know," which Thoreau thought "remarkable, since he had said that he was familiar with the lake." And he chided Polis for huffing and puffing as he climbed Kineo, writing that "perhaps he believed that he was climbing the back of a tremendous moose."

But after hearing the song and having more time to observe Polis, his admiration grew. When Polis and he discussed the phosphorescent wood and other natural phenomenon, he began to see that Polis had a broad understanding of nature, but did not express it in the way a European would. "Nature must have made a thousand revelations to them which are still secrets to us ... . He does not carry things in his head, nor remember the route exactly like a white man, but relies on himself at the moment. Not having experienced the need of the (white man's) sort of knowledge, all labeled and arranged, he has not acquired it."

Thoreau's relationship with Polis is fascinating to follow as the journey unfolds, and occupies a considerable number of the entries in Thoreau's journal. Understanding the native American mind and way of life becomes as central to Thoreau's trip as his contact with nature. Soon the two were sharing knowledge, and both men respected the other's woodcraft. Thoreau even gave a rare verbal compliment after Polis guided the canoe over treacherous waves at the northern end of Moosehead, saying

"You managed that well." And when Polis, who had a sweet tooth, consumed all six pounds of the group's sugar store by filling his cup one third with sugar and two thirds with coffee, Thoreau did not mind purchasing more, even at a north-woods price, from a farmstead on Chamberlain Lake.

My daydreaming, swimming, and soggy-sandwich-eating almost got me stranded on Kineo—I barely made the last shuttle. I told the driver I had started walking to Hardscrabble Point before getting sidetracked by swimming. He said the point had a terrific campsite—if the winds don't kick up. "Just three days ago there were tremendous gusts and some campers had their tent and tarp blown into the lake."

Once back at Rockwood I headed back to Greenville, where I had arranged lodging in an 1890 Victorian home called the Pleasant Street Inn. Innkeeper Sue Bushey has a gem of a place, with a 150-foot wrap-around porch, eight guestrooms furnished with antiques, and a large fireplace in the parlor. The room that really caught my eye was the fourth-floor turret with views of the mountain. I figured such a location would provide inspiration, and I curled up on the couch and scribbled notes from the day's trip.

Whenever I find a region that appeals to me I wonder what it would be like to live there. Would the thrill of new discoveries fade after the first few months? Would the enjoyment of wilderness be replaced by loneliness? Would the long winters do me in? Questions such as these cannot be answered until you actually make the move, stay awhile, and fall into the routine of day-to-day living.

While at the inn I met someone who was doing just that. Susan Veon, who manages the inn when Sue Bushy is not there, had recently moved to the Greenville area with her husband. Previously residing in a Connecticut suburb, she admitted that relocating to northern Maine was a difficult decision, but one they had thought about for years, finally deciding it was now or never.

"Maine advertises itself as the way life should be," said Susan, "and it really is if you like self-sufficiency. We wanted to live here because of the countryside—and because we like the people's attitudes: friendly and helpful. The pace and pressure are different, people are not tied to clocks. They tend to go with the flow a little more readily."

I asked her what surprises had come her way, and she said, "Lots of little things. For example, our house is so far out in the woods UPS won't make deliveries, so we had to make arrangements to pick up packages at the general store. Just to get our regular mail is a forty-minute round trip. But time is one thing we now have and cherish, and you can't put a price on that."

Susan guessed it would take a couple years to assess whether or not the move was the right one. In fact the people she had bought her house from were moving back to Connecticut because there was was not enough work for their construction business. "For us," said Susan, "the important thing is that we give our dream a try."

* * * *

The next morning I left Greenville, taking a roundabout route to reach Interstate 95. Instead of heading directly south, I choose to head west to Jackman via Route 6 and Route 15, then follow the Kennebec River southward to Waterville. The road to Jackman is paved, yet I saw only four other cars in a thirty-mile stretch.

Somewhere along this route I turned off the paved road and onto a dirt road to search for a trout stream shown on my atlas. Big mistake. I never found the stream, let alone the trout, and ended up lost, wondering if a hunter would find my bones come fall. It didn't help matters that when I pulled over to study my map I realized I was parked in the shadow of Misery Knob near Misery Pond in Misery Township.

When I finally did make it to Jackman, I rewarded myself with a cup of coffee and piece of pie in town before launching my canoe on Attean Pond, a scenic lake with over sixty islands dotting four square miles of water. Thunderstorms were moving in so I didn't paddle for long, but I did meet a group of campers who had just completed the "Moose River Bow Trip" which encompasses Attean and Holeb Ponds. They looked like they had been in the woods for months, but they said they loved the three days they spent completing the thirty-four mile loop. Beaver, moose, loons and an eagle were just some of the wildlife they saw. They began their loop journey by paddling westward across Attean Pond, then portaging to Hobel Pond, where they canoed to its outlet, Holeb Stream, which joins the Moose River. Then it was a long paddle down the Moose River, which completes the loop by flowing into Attean Pond.

Having spent the morning lost in Misery Township, I was in no way going to push my luck on Attean Pond, so after exploring its eastern end, I disembarked and continued my trip by car, driving south on Route 201. There is a wonderful view of

Attean Pond from an overlook a few miles down Route 201, but the clouds had the pond socked in, so I didn't stop until I reached The Forks. This little town is aptly named because the waters of the Kennebec and Dead River meet here. Many whitewater-rafting outfits have their headquarters here and generate important income for the regional economy. Class IV and V rapids make this a thrill-seekers paradise, drawing more than 30,000 customers a year. It's a relatively new recreational industry, spawned in 1976 when a fishing guide on the Kennebec noticed that his customers enjoyed the raft ride as much as they did the fishing.

I wonder what Benedict Arnold would think of people paying money to be hurled down an angry river? In 1775, during the American Revolution, Arnold led 1,100 fellow patriots up the Kennebec and Dead Rivers in what they hoped would be a surprise raid on the British at Quebec. Going against the river currents, they dragged heavy, high-sided, double-ended boats called *bateaux* through uncharted wilderness, enduring incredible hardship. Those who survived the trek and the unsuccessful raid probably never wanted to see a river again!

Even if you don't care to go rafting, The Forks is worth a visit because of Moxie Falls. Said to be the highest in New England, the falls are located just west of The Forks off the road to Lake Moxie. A fifteen-minute walk from the parking area will bring you to an observation deck overlooking these remarkable falls.

Flat-water paddlers like me seeking more tranquil water enjoy Wyman Lake, an impoundment on the Kennebec River created in 1920 when Central Maine Power constructed a huge dam south of The Forks in Moscow. The shoreline is largely undeveloped and there are islands and coves to explore.

But on this trip I bypassed both Moxie Falls and Wyman Lake in favor of Houston Falls, located in Moscow on the west side of Wyman Lake. Although much smaller than Moxie Falls, Houston Falls has a beauty of its own, with water cascading over jagged rocks into a shallow pool framed by evergreens. It's a safe spot for swimming, so I waded beneath the falls and let them give me a first-class back massage. I have a tradition of trying to end trips to the north country with a dip into frigid, pristine water. It's my way of saying goodbye, and there is nothing quite like it to make me feel alive.

EXPLORER'S NOTES

Recommended reading

Arundel, by Kenneth Roberts. A fictionalized account of Benedict Arnold's expedition up the Kennebec into Quebec. Roberts' meticulous historical research is woven into this entertaining adventure.

The Maine Woods, by Henry David Thoreau. Read about all three of Thoreau's trips to the Maine Woods. The Penguin edition has an Introduction by Edward Hoagland.

Thoreau's Maine Woods: Yesterday and Today, by Cheryl Seal. The fine writing of this author is enhanced by the photography of Robert Bukaty.

The Wildest Country: A Guide To Thoreau's Maine, by J. Parker Huber. Detailed maps and first-hand accounts of how the land has changed.

Notes on Moosehead

Remember that access to the logging roads, including the Golden Road, is made possible by the generosity of the paper companies. Great Northern Paper Company owns the road and charges a day-use fee of $4 for Maine-registered vehicles and $8 for out-of-state vehicles. Season passes are available, as is camping. DeLorme's *Maine Atlas and Gazetteer* details the Golden Road, as does Great Northern's map sold at checkpoints. Bicycles and motorcycles are not allowed. Information can be obtained from Great Northern's Public Relations office (207-723-2229).

Folsom's Flying Service, in addition to backwoods excursions for sportsmen, offers sightseeing flights that include moose-watch trips and short tours of Moosehead Lake (207-695-2821).

Big Squaw Mountain offers a nice view of Moosehead from its 3,196-foot summit. About seven miles of hiking round trip, and a 2,000-foot elevation change from the base to the top. To reach the trail, drive 5.3 miles north of Route 15 from Greenville. Take a left onto the dirt road directly across from the "Forest Fire Danger Level" sign. Travel a little less than a mile on this road and look carefully for a sign on the right that marks the trail head. (Inquire at the Chamber of Commerce Visitor center for directions and information on other hikes.)

The Wildlife Cruise leaves from Moose River Country Store in Rockwood (207-534-7352).

Maine Guide and Flyshop (207-695-2266).

Wilderness Expeditions offers white water rafting (1-800-825-WILD).

Pittston Farm (call Folsom's Air Service at 207-695-2821).

Lily Bay State Park has excellent campsites along the shore of Moosehead Lake, with running water nearby, a beach and two boat launches (207-695-2700).

The Katahdin Cruises carry up to 150 passengers, who can enjoy both indoor and outdoor seating, sandwiches from the working galley, and narration of the steamship's glory days (207-695-2716).

Moose Safaris (207-695-3054).

The Moose Cruise (207-534-7305).

Moosehead Lake Region Chamber of Commerce, P.O. Box 581, Greenville, Maine, 04441 (207-695-2702).

Winter activities

Moosehead Nordic Center (207-695-2870).
The Birches Cross Country Center (1-800-825-9453).
Moose Country Dog Sled Trips (207-876-4907).
Big Squaw Mountain Alpine Skiing (207-695-1000).
Candeloro Snow Mobile Rental (207-695-3993).

Selected accommodations

Greenville Inn (207-695-2206).
Kineo House (207-534-8812) has six guest rooms, a nine-hole
  golf course, and a restaurant and pub open to the public.
Pleasant Street Inn (207-695-3400).

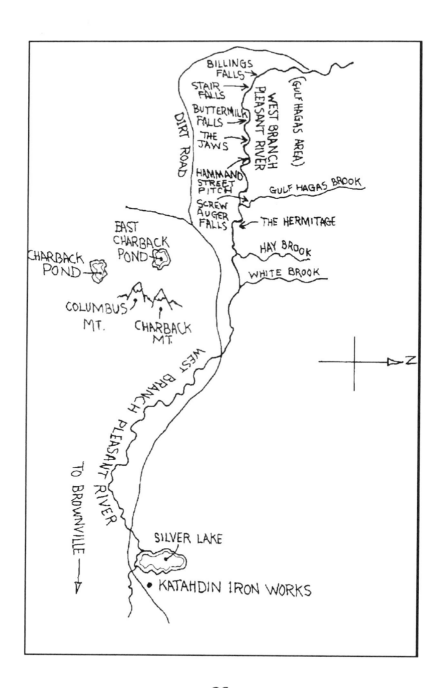

BILLINGS FALLS

STAIR FALLS

BUTTERMILK FALLS

THE JAWS

HAMMAND STREET PITCH

SCREW AUGER FALLS

WEST BRANCH PLEASANT RIVER

(GULF HAGAS AREA)

DIRT ROAD

GULF HAGAS BROOK

THE HERMITAGE

HAY BROOK

WHITE BROOK

EAST CHARBACK POND

CHARBACK POND

COLUMBUS MT.

CHARBACK MT.

WEST BRANCH PLEASANT RIVER

N

TO BROWNVILLE

SILVER LAKE

• KATAHDIN IRON WORKS

The Maine Woods—
Gulf Hagas and the
Katahdin Iron Works

Who you travel with is the most important decision of any trip to the back country. My companion, Cogs, and I have been exploring New England together for so long our trips are "seamless." We know each other's idiosyncrasies and moods, and no matter what situation is thrown our way we seem to handle it with ease. Even "bad" trips are good trips. (Cogs, remember the family of raccoons that moved into my cabin?) We can't always control the events that happen, but we can control our reaction.

Old friends are usually the best friends, because they know you so well they have accepted the whole package of who you are, and each person can be totally at ease. You can speak honestly, even bluntly, and trust that your friend will shed no tears. Suggestions are suggestions, and nothing more. In friendship there is no hidden meaning, and you never measure your words. Humor, even at your expense, is encouraged. Different tastes, different interests, don't mean an impasse, they mean you separate and pursue them. Cogs and I often split up for an afternoon, each fishing a different stretch of river or one person lounging while the other hikes, and then we meet for dinner to trade stories of the day's little adventures. Setting up camp is lounging while the other hikes, and then we meet for dinner to trade stories of the day's little adventures. Setting up camp is done without conversation—you both know what needs to be done and you each set about to do it. There's a division of labor that comes naturally over time.

When we decided to drive to northern Maine after work on a Friday in mid-September, we had no set itinerary—a good practice to follow every now and then. We knew we would hike Gulf Hagas, but that was about all we planned. Neither one of us had been there before, so why make elaborate arrangements and schedules when you have no idea what will unfold? Set your course for adventure rather than destinations and schedules. The wild places will provide you with more thrills than you ever could have planned.

Like so many before us, Bangor was our jumping-off point for the north woods. All three of Thoreau's explorations of the region began and ended at Bangor. Supplies, such as hard bread, pork and coffee would be purchased and packed there, and if a guide was needed a Penobscot Indian would often be enlisted from the nearby village at Old Town. Explorers like Thoreau would board a stage in Bangor for points north and northwest, then proceed by canoe deep into the interior.

Cogs and I arrived at Bangor late at night, finding comfortable lodging at the Riverside Inn, hard by the banks of the Penobscot River. The river and Bangor are relatively quiet now, but up until the 1870s this was the lumber port of the world. Thoreau described the city as "still hewing at the forest of which it is built ... only a few axe-men have gone up-river into the howling wilderness that feeds it."

It was the river that made the city, its waters working around the clock, first carrying logs south from the forest, then powering the sawmills, and finally transporting the larger ships loaded with freshly cut timber south to the sea. The river was never empty; rafts of logs, some a half mile long, floated (frequently jamming) south to the city where mills waited to digest the load.

Bangor's storied past was best told by Stewart Holbrook in *Holy Old Mackinaw:*

"Out on a Bangor street one sniffed the air and found the perfume of pine in it. Bangor was the first city of size whose entire energies were given to the making and shipping of lumber and to the entertainment of the loggers who cut the trees."

For the logger, Holbrook writes that Bangor was nothing less than Paradise:

"Booze, bawds, and battle with roistering loggers—there was really nothing else in life, except timber, and that was handy by. Unwatered rum cost three cents a glass, a glass was a dipperful, and a thirsty logger helped himself with the tin dipper that was chained to the open barrel. And down Exchange Street, a piece, two rather pretty ladies had rented a house and put up a small sign announcing 'Gentlemen's Washing taken In'—a genteel and harmless euphemism. No chamber of commerce was needed to make Bangor: the lodestones were there already and talk in a hundred bunkhouses, back in the deep timber, would take care of the advertising."

If the loggers rollicked, who could blame them, with the inherent dangers in their jobs?

"And die they did," writes Holbrook, "up there in the gloom of the two million acres of tall black stuff—when a sudden waft blew a tall pine the wrong way; when there was the sickening slump in a mile-long landing of logs before they rolled Death over a man; or, the whiskered Old Fellow with the Scythe might hold off, jokingly, until the logs were fair in the stream, then strike you down into the white boiling water of the Ripogenus, on the west branch. Death always stood just behind the logger and very close to the riverman."

* * * *

Everything has changed since those days, from the life of the logger to the Penobscot free of logs. But for the explorer, Bangor is still the edge of the frontier, the gateway to logging country and undeveloped tracts of woods that stretch for mile after endless mile. And it's this lure of the northern forest that has Cogs and me up at the crack of dawn, driving north on the back roads, like Thoreau on the stagecoach.

Just north of Brownville Junction we turn off Route 11 and follow the sign on the dirt road that leads to Katahdin Iron Works and Gulf Hagas, the "Grand Canyon of the East." (Both are part of the Katahdin Iron Jo-Mary Multiple Use Forest, which is another way of saying it's a working forest, where logging and recreation co-exist.) At the ranger station we check in, pay our fee and are lucky to find a campsite still available. A massive kiln and furnace, from the days when iron was produced here, stand across from the ranger station in a field. With my gear is a book about the Iron Works, which I've yet to read, so we decide to hike the Gulf first and return to the site of the Iron Works the following day, after we have read some of the book. Touring historic sites is infinitely more enjoyable when you have read some first-hand accounts of life there.

The trail head to Gulf Hagas lies a few miles farther down a network of dirt roads, and even though we arrive early there are three cars at the parking lot. Word apparently is spreading that this is one of the best hikes in Maine. A trip into the Gulf is an all-day affair, with exploration of the gorge, a patch of old-growth forest, and side trips to waterfalls and swimming holes. We carry in plenty of drinking water, fishing rods and lunch.

The dramatic scenery is largely due to the strenuous efforts of the west branch of the Pleasant River, which drops nearly 400 feet in four miles, carving a passage lined by sheer cliffs and curious rock formations. Hikers of the Appalachian Trail know this gulf as one of the most rewarding pieces of scenery they encounter as they pass through the region, known as the Hundred Mile Wilderness. Bear, bobcat, coyote, moose, deer, porcupine, fisher, and a host of other smaller animals roam the woods.

Just five minutes into our hike we find ourselves removing shoes and socks and rolling up our pants to ford the west branch of the Pleasant River. (The water was only a foot high in the deepest section, but in the springtime, more than one hiker has lost his footing and taken a dunk.) We hike through a second- and third-growth forest of hardwoods and softwoods, then suddenly we are at the Hermitage where virgin white pines tower majestically overhead, some of them 125 feet high. It gives us pause to see such beauty. Imagine if you could hike mile after mile through such timber? There is little undergrowth beneath the cathedral, save for trout lilies, bunch berry, and winter berry, and we feel as though we should speak in whispers among these ancients.

The Hermitage is named for the reclusive Scotsman, Campbell Young, who built a cabin here in 1892, and lived alone on the banks of river for many years. Usually, old-growth stands are found on a steep hillside or ravine, where it was too difficult for early loggers to cut and remove the timber. But this stand is on a flat piece of land right along the banks of the river, making it all the more special.

Most of Maine's old-growth white pine is long gone, having been cut for the insatiable appetite of the ship-building industry that preferred them as mast timber. The pine was so coveted by the British Navy for this purpose that in 1691 the Crown reserved all large trees not growing on private land as their own. This was done with a marking hatchet which hacked out an arrow, signifying British ownership. The British later extended their claim to any size of white pine on ungranted land, and entire stands of trees were cut and shipped to England. After the Revolution the colonists continued the practice, and by the mid-1800s most of the significant stands of pine had been cut and hauled away.

The Hermitage covers only thirty-five acres, so we linger here, moving off the trail to touch one of the largest trees. I let my gaze follow its trunk to the sky, thinking that more and more people are beginning to realize that the old growth has more value to us alive than cut into so many boards. It's as if we have become enlightened but too late to do much good. I think of what's going on in the Pacific Northwest where the fight goes on to protect tracts of old growth, being cut even as I write. Balance. There's got to be balance between the economic needs of the logging industry with a public that increasingly looks at such magnificent trees as part of our natural heritage.

We leave the Hermitage and enter the world of the younger forest, heading westward along a portion of the Appalachian Trail that parallels the river upstream. We hike without talking, falling into an easy rhythm, enjoying the exercise. (I always find it amazing how with each step farther into the woods my worldly concerns recede and are replaced with the here and now.) About an hour down the path we reach Gulf Hagas Brook, where the Appalachian Trail turns to the right, northward toward its terminus at Mount Katahdin.

I've often wondered about attempting to walk the entire Trail. That much time in the woods, focusing solely on your journey, would certainly give you a new perspective on life. But once the trip was over, could you ever go back to the working world? For me it might be the kind of journey to take at retirement, the start of a new life, where doing the Trail might be just the first of many adventures. But I'd never do it alone. The hardships on the trail would be too many to tackle without a companion. (Cogs, are you listening?)

Writers, myself included, often wax poetic about the fun and the adventure of our trips in the woods, which is easy to do when the trips are short. But there's a different side to the forest when you are there day after day—just ask anyone who has hiked for three weeks or longer. Days of dreary rain, wet sleeping bags, blisters and bugs. My hat is off to those few souls who have walked from Georgia to Maine alone—they are made of stronger stuff than me.

Cogs and I follow the branch of the trail that continues straight ahead, crossing over Gulf Hagas Brook, and then turn to the south onto the Rim Trail, following the tumbling crystal-clear waters of the brook. We stop where it plunges down over a ledge into a spectacular waterfall, called Screw Auger Falls. It gets its name from the way the water follows a twisting, water-worn chute that then opens to let the brook pour downward twenty-six feet. At the base of the falls a shaft of sunlight hits the ferns and an aqua-colored pool. For a moment we consider climbing down to cool off, but are lured farther down the Rim Trail to names that beckon: Hammond Street Pitch, The Jaws, Buttermilk Falls, Stair Falls and Billing Falls.

In half an hour we reach an overlook above what we suspect is the Hammond Street Pitch, named by log drivers after a steep street in their beloved Bangor. Sheer slate canyon walls a hundred feet high constrict the river roaring down below.

As we continue down the Rim Trail we encounter two separate groups of lost hikers. Neither group had a map, and one group carried no water. To hike without either is sheer folly, even on well-trod paths such as these. All it takes is a wrong turn on a trail, a few miles in the wrong direction, and then overtaken by nightfall to get novice hikers in trouble. More than one lost hiker has panicked, running in the dark, making the situation much worse. We showed them where they were on our map, gave them water and off they went.

The trail is rugged, climbing, then descending, with roots and rocks to trip you up. A side trail curves back downstream and we take it. Soon the path hugs a narrow ledge above the chasm below, and we need the footing of a mountain goat to keep out of trouble. Down we go into the canyon, rewarded for our effort by a beautiful sun-lit pool. Drenched in sweat and breathing heavily, we shed our clothes and jump in, the cold water slamming the air out of our lungs. We shout with the joy of it, the water washing away the sweat, invigorating us, and reminding us we are still just big kids out exploring. We have crossed the threshold into our forties, but skinny dipping in that freezing water does more than wash the sweat from our skin, it sheds years from our lives. We are ten years old again, whooping and hollering.

The sun dries us on a warm rock ledge, where we devour our lunch. We each have a tiny, ultra-light spinning rod in our packs and cast into the pool. When nothing happens, we carefully make our way downstream, hugging tight to the canyon wall. The downstream pools, darkly shaded by the cliffs, have an altogether different feel than the one we just swam in. The oxygenated water looks perfect for brook trout, but none hit our spinners.

An hour later finds us back on the Rim Trail, where it truly lives up to its name with precipitous drops to the river below, giving me a touch of vertigo when I peer over the edge. Arriving at an overlook above a section of the gorge called The Jaws, we see that it too is aptly named. The walls of the canyon are narrow, constricting the river through an ominous-looking passage. During the days of the log drives, the gap was even narrower. Rivermen dynamited the constriction and increased it to twenty-six feet. But the chasm is a dangerous place no matter what its width—in 1882 a log driver was killed here while trying to free a log jam.

My legs are a bit sore by the time we reach the large, deep pool of water at Buttermilk Falls, and once again we jump in, letting the water work its wonders. With a pair of goggles I dive down toward the bottom, but can see little in the darkness of the depths. If there are giant brook trout here, and there probably are, they are well hidden. We avoid swimming under the falls, where swirling currents have frothed the water, and stay to the north side of the pool.

With all this swimming our hike is taking much longer than expected. Billings Falls, said to be the most spectacular, with three bridal veils of water tumbling into a large pool, is another mile of up-and-down climbing to the west. We discuss the pros and cons of pushing on, but reasoning that we might be hiking out at twilight if we go to Billings Falls, we decide to take a new cutoff trail that connects the Rim Trail with the Pleasant River Road Trail. This will bring us back to Gulf Hagas Brook, where we can swim again.

Pleasant Pond Road is relatively flat compared to the Rim Trail and we breeze along. Thick firs give way to some large hemlocks almost as majestic as the pines at the Hermitage. I pick a sprig of hemlock, crush it and take an occasional whiff, then do the same to a balsam fir, savoring the fresh, pungent fragrance of both. When we arrive at Gulf Hagas Brook we take a final quick dip (knowing there are no showers at the campsites), then hike the last mile to the ford across the river.

* * * *

Our campsite is a beauty, set beneath a huge spreading oak, right on the banks of the river. We quickly pitch the tent, gather firewood, and set up our two deck chairs around the fire ring. It looks as though we are on safari in Africa.

Ducks wing their way up and down the river, and a merganser hunts in the shallows along the opposite shore. Cogs cracks a beer and kicks back, but I'm not done with the water. One last swim. With goggles on, I first swim upstream against a sluggish current, then flip over on my back. I remove the goggles for the slow ride back down, watching the sky and the clouds above. A wood duck flies directly over me, probably wondering about the odd-shaped log floating down the river.

The air has cooled considerably when I scramble up the steep bank to the campsite, and I'm glad Cogs has the fire going. At Gulf Hagas it had reached seventy-five degrees but now it's in the high sixties, and within three hours it will drop to forty-five. Ah, sweet September. Is there a finer month to be outdoors?

We sip our beer, talk about tomorrow, then cook a quick dinner. An owl on our side of the river hoots loudly, and the call is returned from deep in the woods across the water. A million stars shine overhead. I expect to sit with Cogs across the campfire talking into the night, but hiking, swimming and fresh air are more potent than any sleeping pill and he starts to nod off in his chair, then heads into the tent.

It's nine o'clock. I put two large logs on the fire and swing my chair to the side so the firelight will shine on my book, *Katahdin Iron Works and Gulf Hagas, Before and Beyond,* by William Sawtell. I chance across a poem in the Gulf Hagas chapter penned by Leander Coan, titled "A Legend of Gulf Glen." Its first stanza pretty much sums up our day:

If I could paint the North Maine woods,
The sweep of grand old hills,
The bald gray granite mountain range,
The clear moss-bedded rills;
Bring scent of balsam odors here,
Or sounds of forest night,
The soughing wind in tasseled pine,
The glow of camp-fire light;
Or etch the flash of speckled trout
Through deep, clear mountain pool;
Or sketch September sunsets, and
The night air clear and cool;
The relished fare, the hunger keen,
The game-feast spread in camp;
Or slumber deep on scented boughs
After a day's long tramp.

I add a flashlight to my firelight for reading, and learn about the storied past of the Katahdin Iron Works for tomorrow's walk around the kiln and furnace. The night is so quiet it's hard to imagine that just down the road there was once a bustling village with hotel and school alongside the furnaces and kilns that burned and belched smoke around the clock at the turn of the century.

When my eyes grow weary I take a walk down the road. Even though there is no moon, the glittering stars serve as my guide. The trees on each side of the road block out the sky except for a thin strip directly above, so I'm able to stay on the road not by looking down but by keeping my gaze fixed on the dusty heavens. It's a beautiful night with the crisp scent of autumn in the air.

Where the road curves, another smell hits me when the breeze changes. It's a strong odor that can strike terror in the heart of campers. Skunk. Now I wish I had my flashlight, instead of relying on the heavens. A black-and-white-striped hell-raiser might be somewhere near my feet, and I can't see a thing. But I laugh to myself, thinking of my friend Opie, who once spent two night hours trapped in an outhouse when a skunk set up shop at the doorway.

The hoot of an owl fills the sky, and I hope that might scare the skunk. Great horned owls are about the only birds that regularly kill skunks, and I imagine one swooping down to pluck this one for dinner. I also imagine the owl, complete with five foot wingspan, mistaking the top of my furry head for the skunk. I spin around and start back. It occurs to me that walking in such blackness could get me in more trouble than just being sprayed by a skunk. A black bear might use the road for its nocturnal rounds, and its dark coat would make it invisible. Heck, I could walk headlong into a moose and end up seeing more than stars. I can just hear the locals in the coffee shop, "What the heck was he doin' walkin' the road in the pitch dark?"

In spite of my imagination exaggerating the dark possibilities, the night has a beauty all its own, and I refuse to be one of those timid souls that never experience its wonders, always living in a world of eternal, artificial light. I savor the dank, earthy night smells, the haunting sounds from the bark of a fox or a yip of a coyote. Henry Beston, who penned books about Maine as well as *The Outermost House,* often took midnight strolls, and captured the feeling in his poetic prose:

"Learn to reverence night and to put away the vulgar fear of it, for, with the banishment of night from the experience of man, there vanishes as well a religious emotion, a poetic mood, which gives depth to adventure of humanity. When the great earth, abandoning day, rolls up the deeps of the heavens and the universe, a new door opens for the human spirit ... ."

Embrace the forest night—but carry a flashlight.

Back at the camp, I stir the fire and toss on a log, staring into the flames. Bear, fox, coyote and moose—the wildest creatures dance through my mind, and as I think of each I remember warmly the individual sightings over the years that were most special. Seeing wildlife deep in the woods yields memories to last a lifetime. Yet it wasn't long ago that most of the larger mammals, even deer, were becoming quite rare in New England. By the middle of the 1800s beaver had all but disappeared, deer, bear, fisher and martin were scarce, wolves were all but extinct, moose had been pushed back to the interior of the Maine woods, and the spruce grouse was all but gone. All because of the human propensity to change the land, removing every tree of significance, and hunt, bait or trap to the point where continuation of wildlife species was in doubt. The Maine woods became the last stronghold for many of the larger mammals, but even here they were under pressure. To fill the dinner table at the logging camps, moose and deer were shot on sight. Thoreau, during his canoe voyages in the Maine woods, was appalled by the indiscriminate killing of moose, when oftentimes just a few choice pieces of meat were cut from the carcass.

At the turn of the century the public finally began tentative steps toward establishing bag limits, land protection and reforestation. Equally important was the fact that many pastures and agricultural fields were reverting to woodlands as farmers went west. Bear, moose and beaver responded by making a comeback. Moose are now so populous there is a limited hunting season, and a few resident moose are establishing themselves as far south as Massachusetts. The bear population in Maine is over 20,000, although one would never know it because of the reclusive nature of the beast. Deer, which were once so scarce in the north country that Vermont banned hunting for a period in the 1800s, have bounced back in record numbers in most regions of New England. Other species, such as wild turkeys, were later reintroduced in New England and are flourishing. But it's too late for the passenger pigeon, wolves and woodland caribou.

Nature tries to hold on tenaciously, in spite of human encroachment. And when it looses a round, as it did with the elimination of the wolf in the northeast, it adapts, trying a new approach, as evidenced by the arrival of the coyote to fill the void. They were not introduced deliberately, but moved in from the west, or perhaps from Canada where they may have interbred with wolves. However they got here, nature had a niche to fill, and the coyote filled it.

* * * *

When the fire is down to just a few glowing red embers I crawl into my sleeping bag and sleep like a zombie.

Our campsite is perfect in every way except one—it's just a few feet from the gravel road. About six in the morning, a loud whooshing sound roars in my ears, and I think we are about to be slammed by a tornado. I scramble from my bag, and tumble out the tent door, leaving Cogs to an uncertain fate. Then I see it. An enormous logging truck barrels by, kicking up dust in its wake. Cogs continues snoring.

I start the campfire, and rummage around to see what food and cooking utensils we packed. It ain't much. But I'd rather do without a few things than to be like some of the people I saw on the highway who had packed all their worldly possessions into the car, the car-top carrier, and the storage trailer. I want my getaways to be getaways rather than merely moving my home from one place to another. And so I practice a lazy sort of minimalism—bringing the bare essentials, rather than every vestige of suburbia.

A person could easily make a career out of buying all the "necessary" camping equipment and paraphernalia, but they would spend more time in camp, packing and unpacking, and less time walking the woods, floating the rivers, or casting a line to a rising trout. We could have brought a radio, listened to the Red Sox or music (or God forbid, talk radio) but I would not have heard the owl. We could have brought a lantern but then I wouldn't have looked at the stars. We could have camped by showers, but then I wouldn't have floated the river or seen the wood duck.

Too many of us let our possessions own us. They begin to dictate what we do, when we do it, and how we do it. They sap us of creativity, not to mention freedom. The marketing cycle is insidious. We buy more, so we have to spend more, so we have to work more. I'd rather have less stuff and more free time. We are told we need the latest and the newest, even when what we have works fine.

For utensils we have a frying pan, and that's enough. First I make some oatmeal, then Cogs makes fried bananas, tasting as sweet as honey, and we mix them together. The frying pan is then used to boil water for instant coffee. Still hungry, Cogs mentions fried trout, and off we go in search of brookies.

No sooner do we drive away from our campsite than a moose steps from the woods in front of our car. Had the moose crossed our path a second later, there would have been a nasty collision. And that may be an understatement. With their long legs and huge bulk an impact could send the body through the windshield and be curtains for Cogs and me, as it has been for other unlucky souls. But we have time to hit the brakes, and the moose runs away at full gallop. Instead of going into the woods it runs right down the middle of the road, looking left and right for an escape route to its liking.

Later, at a backwater marsh—which I announce is fishless because of the brown water—Cogs catches a beautiful brook trout, resplendent in its fall colors. With marbled back, blood-red spots, and orange-gold belly it is the very symbol of the Maine woods. I quickly put on waders and head into the marsh, every now and then sinking in the muck to a dangerous level. I doubt I would have continued very far if I was alone, but I knew eventually if I sank to my waist, Cogs would come looking for me. (Although I'm willing to bet he would take his sweet time pulling me out, probably snapping a picture or two to show the boys back home. He, being six five, had about as much to worry about from the mud as the moose did.)

About 200 yards into the marsh, small brookies start to take my offering, which encourages me to continue my tramp deeper into the wetlands. There are moose tracks in the muck, and whenever I come to an alder thicket I proceeded cautiously so as not to surprise a bull. Being September I'm not anxious to test the advice I'd been given about bull moose being ornery when looking for a mate. There is other wildlife sign as well. Near a glacial boulder there's a well-used otter slide, and farther down is a beaver dam and lodge.

When we rendezvous back at the car we each have a couple of trout which we store in the cooler. Taking a roundabout way back toward camp, we give the west branch of the Pleasant River a long look, deciding it's worth a try. It's not a particularly large river and the road parallels much of it, but where it pulls away from the road we find solitude, Cogs heading one way and me the other. We fish for a couple hours, learning that the few trout that will venture from their lairs usually come from submerged, tangled blowdowns. We only catch a couple more small trout each, and release them. Cogs, however, tells me he had a decent sized fish rise to his fly where a stream tumbled into the river.

Later, we take a side road toward Chairback Pond. At a height of land a young bull moose steps majestically into the road, framed by rolling mountains mottled with autumn's early color. At each turn in the road a new scene stretches before us, and forest seems to stretch endlessly. But another mile farther we are at a clear-cut logging field where all the spruce and fir have been taken, and only a few hardwoods are left standing.

From seeing a limited amount of terrain its hard to general-ize about the logging practices of a particular timber company. Some show concern for deer yards, soil erosion near streams and steep slopes, while others remove every tree for acres, then spray the new growth with herbicides to keep out the "trash trees," so that a monoculture of single-species trees, all of a uniform age, grow back. Not exactly the diversity essential for a healthy balance of life.

Clear-cutting has been at the heart of the controversy be-tween environmentalist and paper-company interests in Maine, and has received extensive media exposure, particularly the failed 1996 referendum that would have banned the practice. The issues are complex and wide-ranging, and the state unique in that almost half of Maine is owned by private timber inter-ests. Of real concern is the change in forestry practices, driven strictly by the desire to maximize quarterly profits, whereby trees are cut down at an alarming rate, ignoring the more far-sighted practice of harvesting at a pace where the resource is re-newable, diverse and ecologically sound.

Logging has evolved from a seasonal operation where white pine was the primary tree harvested to the industrial forest where mechanization can consume every tree in a tract, leaving nothing to regenerate the forest floor. Development of the skidder and other large harvesting machines, coupled with technological improvements in mills that allow them to con-sume species previously ignored, meant that sections of forest were sheared of all vegetation. Then in the 1970s the spruce budworm infestation promoted even greater clear-cuts, as log-gers moved quickly to salvage dead and dying spruce. When the salvage operations were completed, clear-cutting continued as a standard practice.

Often, the public never sees the destructive harvesting, because beauty strips are kept along the roadways, the Appalachian Trail and rivers. Canoeists paddling down some of Maine's rivers might think they are deep in a virgin forest, when beyond sight the land is stripped bare. The only real way to see the full magnitude of an area's patchwork of clear-cuts is to fly above in a plane. And it's impossible to see the poison spread on the native hardwood seedlings to make way for the single softwood crop.

On the positive side of the timber company equation, think of the enjoyment we explorers have on their land. Imagine for a moment if the timber companies cashed in their proverbial chips and sold the property for private development. Instead of seeing clear-cuts we would see nothing at all. The land would be posted. The wealthy would have their own little sanctuaries and the rest of us would be crowded together in the state and national parks. The solution that must be crafted is one that provides for a productive timber harvest, responsible land management, and access for the public.

A farsighted approach is needed, and that's what so many individuals and organizations (such as the Northern Forests Lands Council) hope to establish development restrictions for the twenty-six million acres of woods spanning New York to Maine. For recreational users like myself, and the seventy million others within a day's drive, the stakes are enormous. Some might call those of us who write about the backwoods and consequently bring more people into the wilds irresponsible. I wrestle with the issue, wondering if I'm walking a thin line between promoting the land to gain more advocates or promoting a land that will loose its very wildness by encouraging more visitors. But ultimately I think that visitors can become more than just curious tourists (as we all are when we first go to a place) and evolve into appreciative stewards who recognize the value of a place that is "unimproved." Traveling is education and awareness, and can spark caring and even action. If you visit a special place that tugs at you and makes your spirits soar, you begin to respect it, to appreciate it, and maybe to even love it. And don't you protect the things you care about?

* * * *

When Cogs and I complete our rambles south and west of Gulf Hagas, we head back to camp and pack up. At the entrance gate we stop at the rangers camp, learn about some of the nearby flyfishing-only ponds, and plan a return trip for next year. Then we cross the road and walk to the kiln and furnace. Standing at the edge of a field with the forest closing in, it's hard to imagine that more than two hundred men worked here during the height of the operation, which included seventeen beehive-shaped charcoal kilns.

The stone blast furnace towers above us and we peek inside, awed by the silent hulk. This was the heart of the operation, where intense heat separated iron from other materials in ore. A mixture of ore, limestone and charcoal was poured into the top of the furnace, ignited at the bottom by a blast of air and heated to high temperatures. To feed this fiery dragon the mountains were stripped of wood to make charcoal in the kilns, one of which is still standing next to the furnace. Fifty cords of wood were loaded into the top of the kiln where a charring fire turned it into charcoal rather than ash.

White settlers first entered this region in 1815 and discovered the iron ore at Ore Mountain, a ridge located just a mile and half west of where we stand. In 1843 the mining and smelting operations began and continued through the 1880s. Because of its isolated location it faced a number of problems associated with transporting the finished product to market. Author William Sawtell notes that transportation amounted to one-third the cost of every ton delivered to Bangor and that it cost six times as much to haul the iron to Bangor as it did to ship it the remaining distance to Boston. To reduce transportation costs a canal was considered, on which barges could float the iron south, but the price tag for constructing one proved prohibitive. Instead, the network of roads was improved both to the south and northward beyond the Iron Works so that teamsters hauling supplies to the lumber camps could return via the Iron Works and haul the iron to Bangor instead of returning with empty wagons.

In 1881 an extension of the Bangor and Katahdin Iron Works Railroad was built from Milo Junction to the Iron Works. In addition to hauling the iron, it had passenger service on a train pulled by a locomotive called the Black Maria. Her maiden voyage was described by writer Marjorie Brockway as a cause for celebration:

"On her first run over the nine miles of gleaming new tracks to Brownville Junction it is said that the Black Maria carried the entire population of KI. Men, women and children made the trip with songs and shouts and laughter in high holiday mood. Although Black Maria chewed up 4,000 cords a year of the precious wood that had to be hauled for longer and longer distances, she well earned her keep. She was almost constantly on the run, carrying out ingots and bringing back supplies, guests and aid when it was needed. In case of accident or illness, she was dispatched to Brownville with whistle wide open. When he heard her screaming around the hill, the doctor in Brownville would snatch up his satchel, sprint to the station and jump aboard the minute Black Maria chugged in."

The Silver Lake Hotel, a handsome three-story structure, was situated on the shores of the lake, only a stone's throw from the kiln and furnace. It was advertised as, "A summer resort for invalids, tourists and sportsmen. The house has accommodations for 75 to 100 guests. It is situated in the vicinity of pond, mountain and forest scenery, in close proximity to the favorite fishing grounds of this region and near the famous Katahdin Mineral Springs. Many a restored invalid would gladly attest to the virtue of its waters."

Apparently the fishing was better then than now, or the advertisements were hyperbole: "Here the stream, in forcing its way down the mountain side, has worn a wonderful gorge, presenting some of the grandest scenery to be witnessed anywhere on the Atlantic slope. White Brook, Hay Brook and the Gulf are all celebrated fishing grounds. No where are trout more abundant than in this vicinity."

The nearby ponds get equally high grades: "And these mountain lakelets all teem with speckled beauties, making this a veritable paradise for sportsmen. Among the more famous of these beautiful sheets of water are Little Houston, Chairback,

Long, Spruce Mountain, Greenwood, and West Branch. Six miles from the Hotel is situated the famous 'gulf' which is reached by buckboard after a delightful drive up."

All traces of the hotel are gone now, and the lake is silent except for the eerie call of the loon, reverting back to its days of seclusion when the natives knew it as Mumolongin, which means "Red Paint Pond" (due to the red ochre found at Ore Mountain).

* * * *

Dusk is falling when Cogs and I leave Katahdin Iron Works, traveling southwest to Dexter, where we spend the night at a delightful bed and breakfast. The Brewster Inn is a nineteen-room mansion, now listed on the National Register of Historic Places. It was formerly the home of Maine's late Governor and U. S. Senator Ralph Owen Brewster. Sitting on a knoll just outside the center of town, it features an expansive garden with a large rose arbor, a perennial-garden pergola with grapevines, and decorative stone walls. Best of all it has a country porch overlooking the garden, where we relaxed on the Adirondack chairs.

I love the stories of how bed and breakfast owners take the plunge into the business or how they happen to end up in a certain place. Innkeepers Bonnie Caswell and Mary Ellen Beal were looking at inns throughout Maine before choosing Dexter as the perfect size of town. In 1987 they saw the Brewster House and "knew it was the one." The home was unoccupied and inquiries into ownership led to dead ends. Finally, on their final trip to Dexter, Bonnie bought a postcard and mailed it to "Resident, 37 Zion Hill Road," and wrote, "I am interested in purchasing your home." Time went by, but she did get a reply and a deal was struck.

"We love small-town living, the people are real neighbors here," said Bonnie. "It's a wonderful experience. Guests explore the North Woods by day, going up through the Moosehead area or KI, and then come back to comfort at night."

Another place guests can go is to Borestone Mountain Sanctuary, owned by the National Audubon Society. It's a great place for kids, because halfway up the mountain is a staffed visitors center at Sunrise Pond with natural history exhibits on display. Children can rest and picnic here before pushing on to the summit, with its 360-degree panoramic views.

I'd hiked the mountain years earlier, and Cogs and I start driving there the next morning. But the day is overcast and getting darker by the minute so we decide to check out Peaks Kenny State Park, which was closer, just north of Dover-Foxcroft. The park is nestled at the southern end of Sebec Lake, and looks like a superb place to set up camp, especially if traveling with children. There is a large sandy beach, swing sets, horseshoe pits, showers, rest rooms, picnic tables and grills. A two-mile hiking trail leads up to the birch mountain ledges.

From the beach, the view north is a wild one, with a jagged mountain shaped like an M in the distance, and a rocky shoreline of spruce, fir, cedar and pine. Wind-driven whitecaps whip across the lake, and I think of all the explorers who fell in love with these lonely hills as I have. I've often felt I was born in the wrong century, that I would have been more at home in an earlier time. And who knows, maybe in another life I was a "timber-hunter" in the Maine woods, setting off in the autumn to search the forests for the large stands of the coveted white pine. Up the Penobscot my companions I would go, paddling our bateau northward, then pushing up a river branch into the interior of virgin forests that had yet to hear the echo of white men's voices. Huge trout, enormous old-growth pines, and forest that stretches all the way to Canada without a single road to mar the land. Everything larger than life. And even now, as I gaze out on the angry gray waters of Sebec lake, I think that northern Maine is still larger than life, still the frontier attracting those with wanderlust and sense of adventure.

EXPLORER'S NOTES

Recommended reading

White Pine and Blue Water, edited by Henry Beston (author of *The Outermost House*) is a collection of some of the best writing on Maine's past. It includes stories of the lumber boom, Bangor, and adventures in the back country.

Local author Bill Sawtell has written a number of historic guides about the region, including *Katahdin Iron Works and Gulf Hagas, Before and Beyond.* Sawtell also leads tours of the Iron Works. He can be reached at 207-965-3971, or P.O. Box 272, Brownville, ME 04414.

The Northern Forest by David Dobbs and Richard Ober goes beyond the issues faced in the north country and lets us understand the people who live and work there.

Selected lodging and campsites

The Riverside Inn at Bangor has fifty-six guest rooms designed and furnished in the style of a nineteenth-century country inn (1-800-252-4044).

The Brewster Inn in Dexter has seven large bedrooms with private baths. We stayed in the "Game Room Suite," which features the original decor of Governor Brewster's private game room. A window seat in the front corner of the inn provides a view of Dexter. Another wonderful room is the Truman Room where President Harry Truman stayed when visiting Senator Brewster. Hanging on the wall is photo and letter from the President thanking Brewster for an enjoyable stay at the Brewster House (207-924-3130).

There are a limited number of campsites at Katahdin Iron Works, but other sites are located about an hour away. One is at Peaks Kenny State Park at Dover-Foxcroft, and another is at Lily Bay State Park north of Greenville on Moosehead Lake. The Maine Bureau of Parks and Recreation operates both.

Old Town Museum in Old Town (207-872-7256) has exhibits on the history of the lumber industry in the nineteenth century.

Gulf Hagas and Katahdin Iron Works

A map of the trails at Gulf Hagas can be obtained at the Ranger checkpoint station. The Maine Bureau of Parks and Recreation (Station 22, Augusta Maine 04333) can be contacted for fees and information. Or you can call the KI Mary-Jo Forest at 207-965-8135 (seasonal).

DeLorme Mapping Company publishes the *Maine Geographic Hiking Guides*. A map and brief narrative can be found in Volume 3 for the Northern Region of Maine.

Special thanks to all those individuals who are working to protect the Northern Forest for both the wild creatures and mankind.

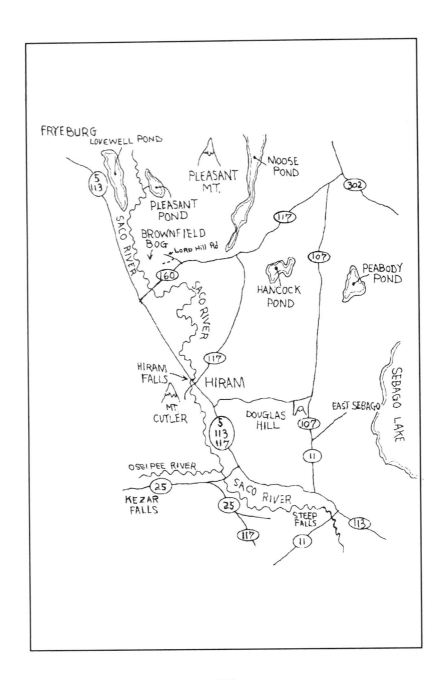

FRYEBURG
LOVEWELL POND
PLEASANT MT.
MOOSE POND
⑤ 113
PLEASANT POND
302
117
BROWNFIELD BOG
Lord Hill Rd
107
PEABODY POND
⑯⓪
SACO RIVER
HANCOCK POND
SACO RIVER
117
HIRAM FALLS
HIRAM
MT. CUTLER
DOUGLAS HILL
EAST SEBAGO
SEBAGO LAKE
⑤ 113 117
107
11
OSSIPEE RIVER
25
SACO RIVER
KEZAR FALLS
25
STEEP FALLS
113
117
11

56

A Week of Rambling in Southwestern Maine— Pleasant Pond, Brownfield Bog and the Saco River

The atlas showed a good-sized body of water adjacent to the Saco River called Pleasant Pond, just North of Brownfield Bog in Denmark. The pond looked isolated with no roads circling it, and the river has a run of six or seven miles with no bridges spanning it. Even though the river looked secluded on the atlas, I'd been warned that this stretch attracts many weekend paddlers. The Saco is simply "loved too much," with its clear, clean water prized by quiet-water paddlers. And it's within easy striking distance of Massachusetts. Timing is everything when seeking solitude on the Saco, so I began my exploration early on a Monday morning in July.

Dawn on the water is a special time and paddlers are usually rewarded with a special sight, but I wasn't prepared for the one I saw that morning. Rounding a bend near the AMC Camp at Walker's Island, I saw enormous dark-colored birds perched at various levels on a riverside tree. From a distance they reminded me of vultures from an old horror movie set in Transylvania.

they were—turkey vultures to be exact. About twenty of them were roosting in a single tree and all kept a wary eye me. Or maybe these carrion eaters were eyeballing me for a different reason.

With large hooked bills, long talons, and red heads that looked like blood atop a black cloak, the birds sent a chill down my spine. In all my years of paddling I'd only seen single vultures high in the sky soaring in wide circles on their daily search for carrion. I had never seen one close-up, let alone twenty giving me the evil eye. The vultures shifted nervously, clearly reluctant to leave their night's perch, and it was only when I glided directly beneath their tree did they flap their way to new positions higher up. They seemed more annoyed than afraid. One in particular looked like its next move would be towards me rather than away.

Their wingspan is about twice that of a broad-winged hawk, and they didn't look much like any other bird I'd ever seen, with their strange naked heads. (They get their name for the red skin on their heads that look like a turkey's red neck.) I took a few photos, expecting them to take flight at the click of the camera. But they didn't move and and never once made a sound. (I later called the Audubon Society and learned that turkey vultures will sometimes roost together in September, but that it was very unusual to see a group together in the summer.)

I paddled silently past, into the mist, changing my focus from the birds to the hypnotic effects of the paddling. Stroke after stroke, I watched the water swirls from the paddle sweep away behind the canoe, like little tornadoes in the ink-black water. From time to time I cast out a Rapala minnow lure, but there were no hits. I knew the fish were there, though. A few years earlier I had paddled the Saco with friends and spent more time floating in the water with a mask and snorkel than I did in the canoe. My friends thought it a bit strange, but I loved seeing all the bass.

Today, I wanted to catch a bass not so much for sport but because I needed a picture. I'd sold a fishing piece to a national outdoor magazine, but payment was contingent on my providing them a quality photo of a bass. I thought it a little absurd that a magazine could like my writing, but hold publication captive to my photographic skills. The magazine in question had turned down a few of the photos I'd submitted, saying the background wasn't right, the photo too dark, or the fish was too small. I could easily do something about the first two problems, but catching a large bass to meet a deadline was something else again. In fact, it was the perfect scenario for Murphy's Law to kick in, and I wondered if I'd catch anything at all. And if I did get skunked, I was beginning to think it would serve me right for fishing for the wrong reasons.

Farther up the river was the creek which led to Pleasant Pond, and I paddled up it, arriving at the pond five minutes later. Pleasant Pond is an apt name. Framed by the peaks of the White Mountains in the distance and with only a cabin or two on its wooded shoreline, it is, at 240 acres, one of the few large ponds in Southern Maine still undeveloped. At one end of the pond is a wide swampy margin, the perfect place for wading birds and wood ducks. I was the only one on the pond, and I later learned from a friend that few people paddle the pond because it's accessible only from the Saco. She also told me that in

October you not only have the pond to yourself but most of the river as well, even on a weekend.

A strange whizzing noise above startled me from reverie, and I looked just in time to see a loon fly by overhead like a bullet. For such a large bird it's amazing how fast they can move. The noise from its wings was followed by a quick tremolo call. From the opposite side of the lake came an answering call, but it was slow, mournful wail. I paddled over for a closer look at the bird in the water. It would stick its head in the water, scouting for fish, then dive, seeming to stay underwater for an eternity. I timed its dives, expecting them to be three or four minutes, but the average was only a minute and fifteen seconds. Then I tried to guess where it would pop up, but it was useless. The loon covered incredible areas of water in those dives, using its feet for propulsion, sometimes surfacing on the other side of my canoe. Later I saw the loon take off. It then dawned on me why I never see loons on rivers or small ponds—they need a long "runway" to get airborne.

Loons are especially handsome birds, particularly when looked at through binoculars, when you can see the detailed patterns covering the head, neck and back. It's amazing the beauty they have in just black and white. The head is solid black, the neck has vertical stripes like a zebra, and the back has white and black checks, larger on the top and tapering to dots at the sides and rear. Many birds and animals have colors to blend in with their surroundings, but the loon seems to have been created with pen and ink, with no thought to the green-blue waters of the lakes it swims in.

I had two more surprises that day. The first was a young mink I spotted prowling the shoreline near where the creek meets the lake. It was a little smaller than a house cat and covered with dark brown hair. There was a stump a few feet out in the water, and the mink slipped into the lake and swam over to it, scrambling up, and then examining every inch. This little creature is a formidable hunter—even the ducks nesting on islands and trees are not safe. I felt sorry for the loons trying to raise their young in nests along the shore or on islands. No wonder the babies ride on a parent's back.

But the mink is part of the natural world and it needs to eat too. More serious problems facing the loons are man-made, especially the increase in motorboating on lakes. The wakes from such boats can drown the eggs in shoreline nests. Lead fishing sinkers are another serious problem. Many loons die from lead poisoning after swallowing the sinkers, perhaps mistaking them for gizzard stones they pick up from the lake bottom.

I paddled out toward the center of the pond for more fishing, figuring I'd try the age-old night crawler drift, letting the breeze push me across the pond. At the end of the drift I was still fishless but heard a splash next to the shore and quickly turned, just in time to see a great blue heron lift its head from the water with a fish in its beak. This was no minnow, but a fat sunfish, and the bird struggled with it. It held it sideways in its beak for a long moment, then flipped it so it was head first. But the fish was simply too big for the bird to swallow whole, and when the heron tried to make an adjustment, the fish fell out of its mouth. It probably would have grabbed the fish again, but the breeze had carried me closer and the heron noticed me for the first time, launching itself into the air. Its first two flaps looked awkward, as if a bird so large was meant to be earthbound. But its awkwardness soon turned to grace, and the prehistoric-looking bird glided away, flying low over the marshy area of the pond.

As I paddled back homeward, I marveled at the wildlife I'd seen, buoyed by the knowledge that even the Saco still had a touch of wildness.

* * * *

The next day I was back in the canoe, this time putting in off River Road below Cornish Station. I brought a small electric motor, which if angled properly allowed me to paddle on the opposite side of the canoe and still keep a straight line when going against the current.

There were no other boats on the water and the only sound was that of a red-tailed hawk that left its perch in a dead pine, piercing the air with its screech. A Kingfisher took off from another perch, flying downstream low to the water. About a quarter mile up, the river split around an island, with a strong current on either side. Even with the motor at full speed and me paddling furiously, the canoe barely made headway, taking me five minutes to go thirty feet. With arms like lead, I cleared the island channel and made my way up to the Route 5 bridge.

Now it was my turn to rest and let the current carry me back down like a drifting leaf. Using a spinning rod, I cast behind rocks, logs and next to the river bank. When the canoe floated back to the island I guided it to the back end and swept into the eddy. In the slack water a fish hit my lure, jumping a good foot into the air. It was a ten-inch smallmouth, its bronze flanks glistening in the sun. I caught two more fish about the same size that were holding in the slack water, then the action stopped.

I paddled back into the current and continued my drift, noting that the hawk had returned to the exact same perch. Floating on the water allows the mind to wander like the canoe's lazy drift, and I put my rod down and lay back on the stern, watching the riverbank. I noticed there were scars on the pine trees about six feet up, and assumed they were from the ice and logs that come hurtling down the river in the spring.

Maybe the logs were coming all the way from New Hampshire's White Mountains, where the Saco rises at Saco Pond above Crawford Notch. From there it dashes southward to Conway, then hooks to the east, passing into Maine. At Fryberg it makes an odd turn back to the north for a few miles then begins a series of looping turns, generally heading to the southeast.

In his book, *Saco Valley*, author G. T. Ridlon writes of the river's tendency to flood, as it is "greatly disturbed by freshets. The water frequently rises ten feet and has reached the height of twenty-five feet, resulting in a great destruction of property along its entire course." It's an interesting book, particularly for historians, and those who have grown up near the river.

"Who that spent their early years on the Saco, that has fished along its banks, sailed upon its surface, bathed in its eddies, or listened to its murmur can cease to look back with pleasure to those careless, happy days?"

Ridlon includes a poem about the river's lure:

Hail! hail again, my native stream,
Scene of my boyhood's earliest dream!
With solitary step once more
I tread thy wild and sylvan shore,
And pause at every turn to gaze
Upon thy dark, meandering maze.
What though obscure the woody source,
What though unsung thy humble course:
What if no lofty, classic name
Gives to thy peaceful waters fame,
Still can thy rural haunts impart
A solace to this chastened heart.

* * * *

If the Saco wasn't going to give up its bass maybe a nearby pond would. (In Maine, just about every body of water that is less than ten miles long is called a pond.) The following morning at Moose Pond, where the state record largemouth had been caught, I had luck working a rubber worm through a weed bed. I landed three fish in the two- to three-pound range, but I had forgotten my camera for the all-important magazine photo. I let the fish go and headed back to Hancock Pond, where I was renting a cottage. I had a few minutes before lunch so I launched the canoe again, paddled to a neighbor's raft and took a half-hearted cast. A fish hit immediately, a very big fish.

My Old Town Pack Canoe is only twelve feet long and it's possible for a bass to pull it a bit, which is exactly what happened. I loosened the drag, fearing the line would snap, and the bass used the opportunity to try and shake the hook with a jump, landing heavy on its side in mighty spray of water. Then it bull-dogged down directly under the canoe, wrapping my rod around the side, and taking more line out in the process. Now I wondered if the drag was too lose so I tightened it. This caused the fish to change directions—he was coming up! I could see the line rising away from the boat and I guessed the spot where he would leap. When he did I got a good long look, realizing that the fish was one of the biggest I'd ever hooked, somewhere in the six-pound range. He crashed back into the water, and using the last of his strength, towed the canoe a few more feet. I forced myself not to fiddle with the drag, figuring the canoe was working better than any reel ever could. Slowly the fish tired, and I brought in the line. I had my boat net far down in the water and guided the fish safely to it.

I finally had my fish—within a stone's throw of the cottage where I was staying! I beached the canoe, put a stringer through the fish's mouth and tied the other end to the dock. My plan was to have my wife take a picture of me and the fish, and then I would let it go.

A half hour later after a quick lunch, my wife, two children and I trooped down the hill from the cottage to get the fish and take its picture. I was giving Mary Ellen detailed instructions on the picture's composition: make sure the fish is in focus, only the lake should be in the background, don't shoot until I'm ready and smiling. Maybe her pictures would come out better than the ones I took that the magazine rejected. I positioned her on the dock so the sun would be behind her, then I went to pull up the fish.

At the end of the stringer their was nothing, nothing but the head of the fish. I was stunned. My wife stood with mouth agape. My son asked if I caught it like that.

It slowly dawned on me that a snapping turtle must have eaten my fish—the fish that was to be in the magazine, the fish I was planning to let go, the only big fish I'd managed to catch in years.

My wife started laughing, and snapped a picture of me holding the stringer with just the fish head dangling.

I wondered if the magazine would use the shot.

* * * *

That afternoon we climbed Cutler Mountain, a good way for me to burn off steam. The trail is a good one for kids, not too steep and not too long, and it took us about forty minutes to reach the cliffs near the top. At the summit there is a ledge facing to the south. Below, the Saco River, dark and slow-flowing, winds through the valley, then curves to the right out of sight, giving the valley the appearance of a large bowl. Around the fringe of the river were various marshes and bogs, reminding me of something a fellow at the general store told me. He said that if I really wanted to see a wild place along the Saco I should check out Brownfield Bog.

The next morning I was at the bog at dawn, letting all my senses enjoy the experience: the rich earthy smells, the sound of bird calls, and soft morning light. A narrow passage of open water wound through the heart of the bog, which stretches for hundreds of low-lying acres on the east side of the Saco River. There were signs of beaver and muskrat, and I scanned the wetlands for moose which are seen here on occasion. I wouldn't

have to worry about motorboats here; there were floating islands, and little side passages of dead water that would only
float a canoe.

It was quiet, so I was careful not to make any noise as I
dipped my paddle and glided off. Over the centuries bogs have
been viewed as spiritual places by some cultures, and I could see
why. There is something soothing about the utter stillness,
something mysterious about the life that thrives here. Floating
mats of vegetation, sphagnum moss, and carnivorous plants
such as the sundew and pitcher plant thrive in the bog.

Of all the plants it's the pitcher plant I'm most on the look-
out for because of its uncommon beauty and the way it catches
insects. The plant has large pitcher-shaped leaves with tiny hairs
inside, making it hard for insects who venture into the leaves to
escape. The insects drown in liquid at the bottom of the leaves,
and the plant digests them. In the summer a single red, nod-
ding flower grows from a tall stalk above the leaves, like a sym-
pathy flower for the deceased insects in the leaves.

Bogs are present wherever surplus water does not drain
quickly and decomposing matter builds up. The surrounding
vegetation pushes from the shoreline, slowly choking off the
open water and filling it with vegetation. Bogs are poor in nutrients and high in acidity, receiving most of their water from
precipitation rather than from streams or springs. Brownfield
Bog, like others in the northeast, supports such unique vegetation as sheep laurel, leatherleaf, cranberries, sweet gale, and bog
rosemary. They are especially beautiful in the fall, with rich,
subtle colors.

I paddled deeper into the bog, passing through a sea of purple-flowered pickerel weed. A great blue heron, with neck crooked and legs trailing, flew slowly over the marsh, and a turtle plopped into the water from a log. At any moment I expected to see an alligator slither down the bank. The whole place reminded me of a trip I took through the Everglades.

Paddling away from the main channel and into the open marsh, I felt like an insignificant dot on the landscape, entering a country of unending sky. Not a good feeling, and not necessarily a bad feeling, but a feeling of aloneness that comes in wild, open spaces.

EXPLORER'S NOTES

Canoeing

Avoid the Saco River on weekends in the summer if you like elbow room. Instead, come during the week or in the autumn, and check out some of the less visited sections of the river. The AMC *River Guide to Maine* reviews some great float trips.

Pleasant Pond is fairly shallow, with a maximum depth of fifteen feet. Chain pickerel and white perch are the primary fish, although there are some smallmouth bass. Fore more information and for fire permits, call the Maine Forest Service at 207-657-3552 or 207-287-2275.

Brownfield Bog is managed by the state. It can be reached from the intersection of Routes 113 and Route 160 by taking Route 160 toward Denmark. You will soon cross the Saco River, and you should then go about one and half miles before turning left on Lord Hill Road. About a tenth of a mile down you will see the entrance road into the bog on the left. You can follow this about eight tenths of mile to a launch site where there is a shed with rules posted on it. If the road is not too muddy you can continue past this first launch, bear left at the fork a third of a mile from the shed, and launch about a mile further.

Canoe rentals and camping

River Run Canoe Rental in Brownfield offers camping, canoe rentals and shuttle service (207-452-2500).

Camp and Canoe, Woodland Acres Campground, Brownfield (207-935-2529).

Saco Bound (603-447-2177).

Hiking

The Mount Cutler trail head is located in Hiram. If you are coming from Fryberg south on Route 5, turn right onto River Street just before you reach the bridge spanning the Saco River at the junction of Route 117. Go down River Road a short way and turn right beyond a construction company, then, 200 feet beyond, turn left and park by the railroad tracks. The guide *Nature Walks in Southern Maine* reviews Mount Cutler as well as thirty-nine other walks.

In addition to hiking Mount Cutler, another easy hike is Douglas Mountain in Sebago. From Route 107 take Douglas Hill Road to the west for eight tenths of a mile then left onto Douglas Mountain Road to reach the trail head. From the stone tower at the summit there are great views of the White Mountains and Sebago Lake.

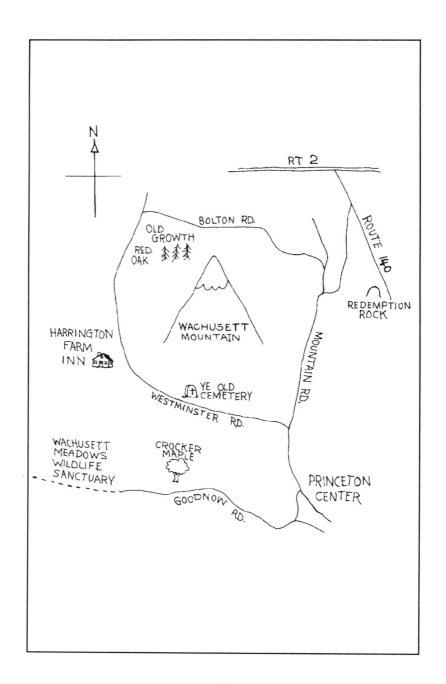

N

RT 2

ROUTE 140

BOLTON RD.

OLD GROWTH
RED OAK

WACHUSETT MOUNTAIN

REDEMPTION ROCK

HARRINGTON FARM INN

YE OLD CEMETERY

WESTMINSTER RD.

MOUNTAIN RD.

WACHUSETT MEADOWS WILDLIFE SANCTUARY

CROCKER MAPLE

PRINCETON CENTER

GOODNOW RD.

Thoreau's Wachusett

The forest lived up to my expectations. Here was a place where elves could live and fairies dance. Enormous red oaks towered above a sparkling stream, whose course I followed, hoping to feel the full magic of an old-growth forest. Thoreau would have loved it here.

It was late November and I was on the north side of Wachusett Mountain, hiking along Bolton Brook. I visited this section of Wachusett first because if I were to find Thoreau—and I considered Wachusett his mountain—this would be the place. He who loved trees would have appreciated a little ravine that had escaped the axe for over a hundred years.

Walking, I marveled at how the oaks had managed to dominate the area; only a couple of other species grew within sight. I touched the rough trunk of the largest oak, wondering if its strength and power would carry into my fingertips. Ahead, the brook called to me over a series of little ledges. A dank, rich aroma of green ferns, growing among the orange-brown of fallen leaves, filled the air.

When the forest loads your senses you can be taken by a singular joy. It doesn't happen often, and you cannot will it upon yourself, it comes in its own time. When it does occur you find you're stepping lighter, seeing more clearly, more vividly, and you move slowly. You feel like smiling, maybe singing. You feel young. I call the sensation a "soaring of the spirit," and for me it only happens in the woods or on the water. It was happening to me now.

Up ahead was a bowl-shaped depression where the sun hit squarely on a tree trunk; a perfect place to sit and wait for Henry. In Thoreau's essay, "A Walk to Wachusett," he makes no mention of a mountain stream, nor does he chronicle a trip to the northern slope. But the *spirit* is not limited to past footsteps or historic bounds. Our shared spirit sought the wildness left in native land, and here was a patch that would make him smile.

So I waited, absorbing the little warmth left in the autumn sun, letting my thoughts wander. Why, I thought, did I not do this more often? It felt so good to be alone in the woods, good to feel tired after walking in the bracing autumn air. It's what we were meant to do—this walking—and my mood responded to the simplicity and naturalness of the day.

Thoreau walked a minimum of four hours *per day* to preserve his health and spirits. He took pity on his fellow Concord neighbors who were house- or shop-bound, wondering how they kept their sanity.

"I confess that I am astonished at the power of endurance, to say nothing of the moral insensibility, of my neighbors who confine themselves to shops and offices the whole day for weeks and months, aye, and years almost together. I know not what manner of stuff they are of ... ."

Sitting in the woods, I felt what he meant. The simple exercise, the silence, the forest air allows you to lose yourself in a sense of well being.

My eyes soaked up this little kingdom. An ancient stone wall ran along the top of the hill, a reminder that in Thoreau's day eighty percent of New England's landscape was cleared for agriculture and pasture. Shortly after his death the trend changed: farmers went west for the stone-free prairies, and in New England the trees reclaimed the fields. Today more of our land is wooded than cleared: one of the few changes Thoreau would have approved of.

Without the overhead canopy of foliage the woods were bright, cheerful, and the orange-brown oak leaves covered the hillside like down, ready to insulate the earth for the coming winter. A lone, massive hemlock had fallen across the stream, its life work over. On the ridge top was the light gray trunk of a beech, some of its yellowed leaves stubbornly clinging to branches. The scene was easy on the eyes, and I lay back, knowing this might be the last time I would feel the sun's rays till spring.

I must have dozed, for when I opened my eyes again the woods were in shadow, their enchanted quality chased away by dusk and a chill in the air.

It was too late to climb the mountain, but that felt right, too. Perhaps, I thought, Wachusett was not to be approached so directly. Thoreau spent many years just looking at the "blue wall," fearing that once he climbed it the mountain's magic and grandeur might diminish.

"At length ... we resolved to scale the blue wall which bounded the western horizon, though not without misgivings that thereafter no visible fairyland would exist for us."

Maybe I should approach the mountain as Thoreau did, from the east. The journey, not the destination, should be the important thing. I would start at Concord and head for Wachusett's distant outline, enjoy its charms from afar before the more intimate climb. Yes, mountains are like some people, not to be rushed.

* * * *

A week later I sat at my kitchen table, topographical maps spread before me, trying to guess Thoreau's path. I searched for the less-travelled country roads, keeping an eye out for streams that held the promise of trout. I saw Henry and his friend Richard Fuller travelling west out of Concord on a cool July morning, passing through Acton and into Stow, enjoying the sounds and scents of open fields and dank woods, then on into Lancaster, where they rested on a hilltop reading Virgil during the heat of the day. They continued walking until nightfall, not stopping until they reached the Stillwater River, just five miles from Wachusett, where they took lodging at an inn.

The following morning, a Sunday, I loosely retraced their steps by car, poking along through still-sleeping towns, seeking the outline of Wachusett to the west. In Lancaster the country opened up a bit, suburbia in its early stages with a few farms stubbornly hanging on between half-million-dollar homes, set back behind stone walls and fenced driveways. On a narrow road that hugged a ridge I got my first good view of the mountain. Just as promised by Thoreau it appeared as a blue wall, a deeper blue than the sky above.

A few miles to the south sprawled Wachusett Reservoir, a lake created to meet Boston's need for water. In Thoreau's day the area was a sleepy little valley of mills and farms. I'm sure he would have disapproved of the reservoir, might have said, "let Boston drink from the harbor." The power of the state—to take the land of the few so that the many could have water—would have troubled him deeply. But the situation does have a touch of irony, which Henry would have loved. In creating the reservoir the state had to protect its watershed, and now there are acres of undisturbed forest along its shore, forming a pocket of wilderness in a region otherwise under development pressure.

The closer I got to the mountain, the more I wish I had company. Old friends and I were drifting apart—the two I had invited to join me today planned to squeeze in one more round of golf before winter. Perhaps walking in the woods was not the tonic for them as it was for me. Perhaps they felt Wachusett was not a challenge and challenge was what they were used to.

It's true the mountain, at 2,006 feet, is small by most standards, but because of its solitary nature it seems bigger. Geologists say that in the beginning Wachusett may have been as tall as the Himalayas, but through millennia of erosion only the more resistant granite rock remains. Because it rises from the flat plains below, it has long been a focal point in the region, or as Thoreau wrote, "Wachusett, who like me, Standest alone without society."

During King Philip's War the native tribes had a large camp at the foot of the mountain from which they launched raids on the settlements to the east. Lancaster was hit hard in the winter of 1676 and many settlers were taken captive. Among them was Mary Rowlandson, who chronicled her hardship (as well as that of the natives) in her book, *The Narrative of*

the Captivity and Restoration of Mrs. Mary Rowlandson. Her
book is a testimony to her faith in God, and to her own physical endurance, as she and her captors crossed from Wachusett
to the Connecticut River and back again.

In addition to her courage, Rowlandson's survival was aided
by a bit of ingenuity. She made herself less of a burden to the
natives by knitting them items of clothing, even though all the
while she was starving, and suffering from the loss of her own
children. She writes of meeting Philip (the leader of the upris-
ing) and tells of making a cap for his son. Later he repaid the
favor, as Rowlandson describes in this paragraph:

"At last, after many weary steps, I saw the Wachusett hills,
but many miles off. Then we came to a great swamp through
which we travelled up to the knees in mud and water, which
was heavy going to one tired before. Being almost spent I
thought I should have sunk down at last and never get out; but
... Philip who was in the company came up and took me by
the hand and said: 'Two weeks more and you shall be a mistress
again.' "

Now, on my drive, I thought of Rowlandson, could picture
her in tattered clothes at the place of her release—a huge, flat
boulder near the base of Wachusett called Redemption Rock. I
thought of all the people who pass right by Redemption Rock
and don't know the story of this remarkable lady. Even sadder,
I wondered if many people knew, or cared about, the native
Nipmucks, Wampanoags and Narragansetts who risked all to
wrestle their country back from the white invaders. Thoreau,
though, knew of these past events, writing, "This, it will be remembered, was the scene of Rowlandson's capture ... . We do

not imagine the sun shining on hill and valley during Philip's War."

Yes, Wachusett is a small mountain, but rich in history, rich in Thoreauvian lore. Maybe today I would find him. Maybe it was best I was alone. Thoreau recognized that the size of a mountain had nothing to do with what it can mean to those that love it:

"It is but nineteen hundred feet above the village of Princeton, and three thousand above the level of the sea: but by this slight elevation it is infinitely removed from the plain, and when we reached it we felt a sense of remoteness, as if we had traveled into distant regions."

I'm sure Thoreau climbed the mountain from the eastern side, and I would too, as soon as I circled its base. I wanted to see it from all sides, all angles. Passing through Princeton center, I thought, "Here is a place I could live." With the mountain for a neighbor, and a town green that seems frozen in time, Princeton has all the ingredients of a first-class New England town.

In the 1800s Princeton was a tourist town where Bostonians would come to escape the suffocating city for the fresh mountain air. Eight trains a day brought visitors (some famous like Thomas Edison, Louisa May Alcott and John Greenleaf Whittier) to the dozens of fine Victorian hotels scattered round the hills.

On impulse I decided to make a short visit to Wachusett Meadow, an Audubon property that has a wonderful old road similar in appearance to the ones Thoreau would have traveled. The road is closed to traffic, and lined by a stone wall crowded by big maples, hickory and beech. As I strolled down the road my eyes were on the the smooth gray trunks of the beech trees. Even though this isn't really black-bear country, I cannot help but scan the tree bark for claw marks left by bruins that scale the beeches for their nuts. Once you see one of these creatures in the wild you never forget it, and if the "meeting" went well, as mine did years ago, you look for signs in hopes of seeing another.

I walked about a mile, then retraced my steps and entered a field where a sugar maple, said to be 300 years old, stood like a benevolent king guarding the peaceful valley. I sat beneath the king, glad to be in the presence of a life that spanned Thoreau's day into my own. The Crocker Maple, as its called, is battered and bruised, with its top sheared off, and two-foot-wide mushrooms grow from its ragged bark. On one side two huge, twisted and gnarled branches sweep low to the ground as if to grab you. In fact, the tree reminds me of the dark and mysterious apple trees Dorothy and the Scarecrow encountered in *The Wizard of Oz*. You may recall how those trees suddenly slap Dorothy's hand and scold her for a taking an apple. The Crocker Maple decided I was harmless, did not reach out and grab me, so I paid my respects and pushed on.

Back in the car I drove along the west side of Wachusett, soon stopping to wander about an ancient graveyard nestled in a hollow below the road. One of the headstones, that of Jonas Harrington, age seven, caught my eye.

Death, like an overflowing stream
Sweeps us away, our lifes a dream

An empty tale, a morning flower
Cut down and withered in an hour.

One might think the haunting words an inappropriate choice of reading on such a fine autumn morning. One might think they would depress me on my solitary journey. But they did not. The contrast between the grimness of early American life and my own sense of gratitude at being in the woods gave me pause, gave me balance, gave me perspective. The air seemed a little purer, the golden woods more beautiful than before. Every day a gift.

I continued my journey, pleased that the woods rolled down the mountain to meet the road. Ahead I could see a series of windmills that turned in the breeze, and wondered what Henry would have thought of them. On the one hand there was no doubt of their ugliness, their giant white blades an intrusion on the forest of green, but they did provide a pollution-free source of energy. I suspect the whole concept of energy—hydro, fossil fuels, solar, and even windmills—would have stirred Thoreau to comment on *us* rather than the energy *per se*. He might have addressed the problem in one word: simplify.

This was my first trip to the back side of the mountain, and I was liking it more and more. The roads were narrow, with potholes, keeping traffic to a minimum, and I hoped they would never be "improved." An old farm-style inn lay at the rise of a hill, and I pictured this as the kind of place where Henry lodged before scaling the mountain. The Harrington Farm Country Inn was built in 1763, and there was something heartening about the way it had been preserved, keeping a worn yet solid look, without calling attention to itself.

Cruising northward, wondering if the Harrington in the graveyard was any relation to the people who founded the inn, I saw a man coming down a mountain path that intersected the road I was on. I waved, he waved back, and I stopped the car and asked him about the trail he had been on. He surprised me by saying he had walked it from the Audubon property, Wachusett Meadow, all the way to the summit of Wachusett, and was now on his way back. It was only 11 a.m. and I estimated he had already covered about ten miles, with some fairly steep climbs.

I commented on the distance he had travelled and he said he made the walk frequently, that he loved the solitude of Wachusett. I shut the car off as he described the wildlife he had seen over the years and how this side of the mountain had remained pretty much as it had been in his boyhood. We talked awhile longer, and when he realized I had no map of the mountain trails, he gave me his own. Then he nodded goodbye, crossed the road, and vanished into the woods.

As I traveled through Westminster, the sun hit squarely on the mountain laurel that lined the road, making their waxy leaves glisten and sparkle. Hemlocks grew thick, signifying that I was in rough country. I completed my loop of the mountain and parked at the base of its eastern side. A road now goes to the top of Wachusett, but thankfully it was closed for November. There is something disconcerting about hiking up a mountain, only to find carloads of tourists at the top. The trail I chose wends its way to the south a bit, gradually climbing, then turns and goes straight north to the mountaintop. It's only a forty-five minute walk, but after just ten minutes my breathing was labored and I concentrated on the rocks below my boots. A man passed me, which is not unusual, except that this one carried his two-year-old son in a backpack, making me wonder what kind of shape I was in.

I kept my eyes on the trail directly below me, enjoying the rhythm of placing one foot in front of the other in methodical fashion. Soon, it seemed, I was in a trance, focusing solely on breathing, stepping and rocks below. This inadvertent meditation is one of the reasons that real climbers have such a love of mountains; the act of climbing becomes a spiritual pursuit, a way to cleanse the soul.

Out of breath, I stopped at an overlook and stared southeastward toward Concord. Thoreau's physical stamina must have been impressive. He not only hiked up mountains, but covered considerable ground just getting from Concord to a mountain. One remarkable solo trip of his occurred in 1844, two years after his walk to Wachusett. At the time his writing career was not going particularly well and he had to support himself by working at his father's pencil factory. Then, things got even worse when he accidently let a campfire get out of hand that quickly torched several hundred acres in Concord. He must have decided it was time for some serious thinking, time to cleanse his soul, and he looked to the mountains.

He put a few items in a pack and left Concord, first going north to Mount Monadnock in New Hampshire, where he slept on the summit. Then he headed westward, crossed the Connecticut River, and followed the rugged terrain along the Deerfield River into the Berkshires. A week passed before he finally arrived at Mount Greylock, the tallest peak in Massachusetts. Amazingly, he bypassed the trails that led to the summit, deciding to use his compass and bushwack to the top. He spent the night on the windswept peak, placing wooden boards on himself in an effort to ward off the cold, and claimed to have slept comfortably. By now, most people would have been exhausted, and headed back home. But Henry met a friend in Pittsfield and continued his journey into New York State, following the Hudson down into the Catskills.

And here I sat, winded and sweating from a twenty-minute climb. But it was a good climb, and probably as therapeutic as tackling a taller peak. Thoreau may have used Wachusett for his own kind of therapy—a diversion from the depression he suffered after the death of his brother John just six months earlier.

Travelling, exercise, mountains: they all have the power to help ease us in troubled times.

On the final leg of the climb, with the sun at my back, the woods of scrubby oak took on a beautiful look. I looked west through the bare trees and was mesmerized by the blue haze along the horizon. Sensing I was near the top, the spring came back in my step, and I almost ran the last hundred feet. I arrived panting, feeling great, as if having done penance before entering this sacred place.

A broad panorama lay before me, not spectacular as the state brochure claims, but still impressive. My eyes went not to the skyscrapers of Boston, but rather to the dark outline of Mount Monadnock to the northwest, nature's creation more arresting than man's. A breeze blew over the summit, making me feel small and insignificant. Henry described it as "a place where gods might wander, so solemn and solitary, and removed from all contagion with the plain." I could see him sitting by his tent with a huge bonfire casting eerie shadows. I saw him look to the sky, thinking of his brother, and marvel at the stars, which he thought were "given for a consolation to man."

I could see him, but no words came to me, and I let my mind drift again. I thought of the hiker who gave me the map and disappeared into the woods. He could have been Thoreau reborn, so certain was he in his element on his solitary trek through the woods. I wondered at the power of this mountain to bring Henry's spirit back in such a man.

I sat there quite awhile. A mountaintop is a good place to sort things out, the pure air and long views assisting the thought process. My problems were small ones. Perhaps they were the beginning of a mid-life crisis, where you know the journey of life is more than half over and you feel a sense of urgency to somehow *do more*.

The sun was going down, but I didn't want to leave. I stared westward toward indistinct hills where I grew up. A lone hawk circled above, dark against a sky which now had a touch of pink. Earlier in the fall there might be hundreds, even thousands, of hawks, ospreys, falcons and eagles circling in the skies, but now the single hawk was perfect for my mood.

I was not solving my little problems, could not focus on a single one, so I stretched my legs and prepared to go. Maybe I would just leave my worldly cares on the summit—the wind was sure to pick them up and blow them away. I'd let the wind sweep away the clutter and I'd focus on the important things.

Sometimes, I said to myself, the simple solutions are the best. *Simple, simplify?* Where had I heard that before?

EXPLORER'S NOTES

Recommended reading

Thoreau's natural history essays, such as "A Walk to Wachusett" and "Walking," are among his best work, showcasing his keen eye for nature in combination with a spiritual quest.

Henry David Thoreau: The Natural History Essays is a compilation of several of Thoreau's essays by Gibbs Smith Publisher.

Nature Walks in Central Massachusetts, by Rene Laubach and Michael Tougias, published by the Appalachian Mountain Club, gives descriptions of a hike up Mount Wachusett and a walk at Wachusett Meadow.

Related information

Wachusett Mountain State Reservation (508-464-2987) has a nature center, hawk migration information and trail maps. The recent attention on the old-growth section of forest alongside the ski trails should not overshadow the other old-growth stand of red oaks at the park's northern end, which is protected by the Department of Environmental Management's Wildlands Program.

Wachusett Meadows Wildlife Sanctuary in Princeton gets my vote for the best Audubon property in the state (508-464-2712).

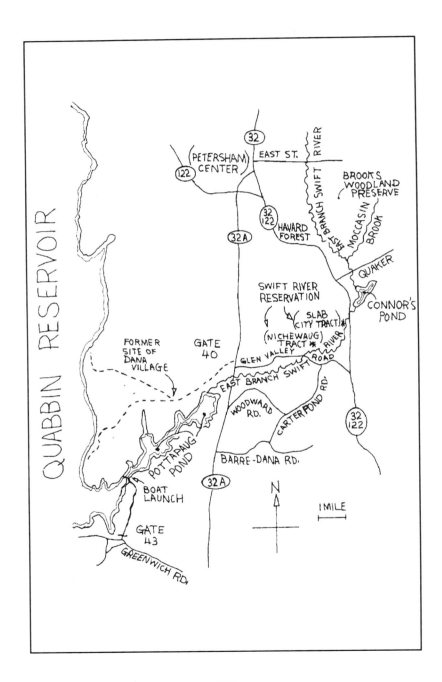

The Last Wilderness—
Quabbin Reservoir

The snow keeps coming and we walk on, heading deeper into the white forest. Like ten-year-old boys we love the snow, love the pure magical quality it gives the woods, and feel the excitement of knowing ours are the first human tracks to walk the old road that December day.

Large fluffy flakes float down in still air. All this motion and no sound. Maybe that's why some of us are drawn to snow, wanting more when others say "enough." My brother Mark and I draw energy from the flakes, and the call of Quabbin is strong.

Now we turn off the road and pass beneath the hemlocks, following fresh deer tracks. At the top of a small knoll we stand silently and Mark spots a doe at the bottom of the south-facing slope. Soon we see another, and then later a third, suspecting that there are many more just out of sight. The deer yard covers several acres, and season after season the deer congregate here when the snow is more than a foot deep.

We push on, gliding toward the reservoir like ghosts. With the new fallen snow we can move through the forest as quietly as the creatures that call this wilderness home. Coyotes, bald eagles, fisher, fox, beaver and porcupines—over the years we had seen them all at Quabbin. And we wonder if the reports of a mountain lion could be true—there are certainly enough deer to support one.

By the time we reach the reservoir, the snowflakes have lost their size but increased in number, hissing as they hit our parkas. The broad shoreline looks like tundra, and the reservoir itself seems a void of white, swirling space. A bit of wind asserts itself, and as it whisks across the frozen surface, mini-tornadoes of snow appear, not unlike the "dust devils" on the desert. But this is no desert; beneath the thirty-nine square miles of ice on the reservoir there teems a fishery that is perhaps the best in the state.

Located in Central Massachusetts, Quabbin has been referred to as the "accidental wilderness" because the creation of the reservoir meant the surrounding watershed had to be protected, forming a wildlife refuge of 120 square miles. But before the forests, before the reservoir, the land was home to the citizens of four towns.

Created in the 1930s, Quabbin was a curse to those who lived in the Swift River Valley. Imagine owning a farm here before the reservoir, struggling to eke out a living from the bony soil. Imagine seeing engineers, tramping through your fields, taking measurements, making calculations. Then the rumors follow, and you shake your head in disbelief: flood the valley so Boston could have water? Preposterous. But land prices plunge anyway.

Soon the politicians come, and together with the engineers they tell the farmers that the Swift River Valley has all the necessary characteristics for a huge reservoir. The clear-flowing rivers are exceptionally clean and the surrounding hills would be perfect for walling in the water. They do not mention that the valley also has another necessary ingredient: no political clout.

The residents of Enfield, Greenwich, Prescott and Dana are stunned: their towns are to be wiped off the face of the earth, swallowed up by a reservoir that will be the largest man-made domestic water supply in the world. Angry citizens fight back, and the battle goes all the way to the Supreme Court. But Boston wins, and by 1939 the homes that had been in families for generations are razed, the mills destroyed, the forests logged. Even the dead can not rest in peace: 7,500 bodies are removed and reinterred at a state cemetery.

A 2,640-foot-long dam, named the Winsor Dam after the chief engineer, is completed, as is the smaller Goodnough Dike. The river's path is now blocked, and its waters rise, spreading over fields, cellar holes, and roads, obliterating all signs that this was settled land. For seven years the reservoir expands, until 400 billion gallons fill the north–south valley, turning a number of hills into islands.

Now Mark and I look out through the falling snow, knowing that those islands are out there, off limits to humans. Mount Pomeroy, Mount Lizzie, Mount Zion, and others, they are mysterious places where eagles roost and coyotes hunt.

On past hikes I'd seen both predators far out on the ice, picking over the carcass of a deer that made the error of trying to flee on the slippery surface. The eagle is an opportunistic hunter in the winter, feeding largely on carrion, but the coyote uses the advantage of pack hunting, wearing down a swifter prey. More than once I've spotted a long line of the "little wolves," trotting single file on the ice, and wondered what creature they were tracking.

Mark decides to walk the shoreline, disappearing into the dim grey light, as if passing through a curtain to a different world. I brush snow off a log and sit.

Silence. Perhaps I've never experienced such utter quiet, such complete absence of distraction. I write in my journal, hear pen scratching on paper, before the flakes dampen the page. The snow envelops me, and lonely feelings come with it, a feeling of penetrating loneliness. The exact notes from my journal read: "The silence is so strong it feels like a force, a pressure, wrapping completely around. It insulates and isolates; I'm the only person on the planet."

Quabbin has the power to make you feel part of nature itself, to humble you. Still, it's good to know that there is a place where one can go to be alone, where the snow can fall in peace without the sound of cars, snowmobiles, or other voices. As the urban sprawl spreads west from Boston, Quabbin stands as the last wilderness.

Some wonder why I would write about a place that is so special—won't my love of the place be its undoing, won't others come? I do not worry; walking these roads is not for everyone. Even now the Quabbin receives over 250,000 visitors annually, but most of them confine their activities to the area around the dams or focus on fishing. There are not many of us who come simply to walk.

In fact I believe that the few walkers will someday become the Quabbin's guardians. As time goes on, the demands to use Quabbin as a recreational area will certainly increase. Long ago the anglers used their influence to open up its waters for low horsepower outboards, and astronomers were allowed to build an observatory on Prescott Peninsula, which had been set aside for wildlife only. If we allow the politicians to run the place they will try and make everyone happy, and loons will be replaced by jet-skiers, and the last wilderness will be no more.

As I sit on the log it occurs to me that Quabbin is nothing more than the rivers and streams that feed it. In fact the name Quabbin is from the Nipmuck Indian word meaning "place of many waters." The rivers are the arteries of this special place, perhaps the soul.

In my efforts to "know" Quabbin, I've come in all seasons, hiked down most of the access gates, and spent countless hours looking over its blue waters. But I know little about the three branches of the Swift River that fill this liquid bowl. The East Branch of the Swift is particularly appealing, passing through a number of reservations where a person can walk all day and not see another soul.

Now I wish to know that river, follow it closely, see the exact location where its current ends and the Quabbin begins. The very idea, fascinates me—rivers can do that.

* * * *

It wasn't until April that I got around to exploring the East Branch of the Swift. My plan was to have a "walkabout," a whole day in the woods, walking from dawn to dusk, with the river as my companion. I even had the good fortune to hear about an excellent bed-and-breakfast nearby, where I would spend the night after my walk. Then on the following day I hoped to explore the back roads and villages which looked so inviting on my atlas.

The day of the walkabout was chosen to coincide with my thirty-ninth birthday. It was my wife's idea. Long ago Mary Ellen understood my need to balance society with being alone, and this was part of her birthday gift to me. It might seem a rather odd way to spend a birthday, but for me it was perfect. Time—quality time, without feeling hurried—is something I seek on a regular basis. In a world where what we do, when we do it, and how long we do it, is seldom set by ourselves, a walkabout restores a bit of balance. Now I would have two days to poke around one of my favorite places, and let the peace of Quabbin turn back the inner clock a few years—or so I hoped.

My need for occasional solitude should not be confused with those who seek to cut off all ties with people. On the contrary, after a few days in the woods I've had my full, am ready for the stimulation of the company of others. "When tired of trees I seek again mankind," wrote Frost.

Thoreau said it differently: "Be a Columbus to whole new worlds within, explore the ocean of one's being alone." This has led some to refer to him as a hermit, a recluse. Nothing, however, could be farther from the truth. Even while living at Walden Pond he made many visits to town, often joining his family for dinner. And the door to his cabin was open, welcoming those who wished to visit. No, Thoreau and Frost were no different than many others, they merely did a better job articulating the spiritual benefits of spending some time alone.

Few material gifts would mean as much to me as this opportunity for a two-day ramble. The length of a journey is not the essential ingredient. Whether it is a year, a month, or just a day, a true journey is one where the spirit coincides with the place. Many travelers go off for months, sprinting from point A to B, then on to C, visiting the "sights," but never seeing, never feeling. Some check off their various destinations like items on a grocery list, while others collect postcards in lieu of notching their belts.

On the drive to Quabbin I thought about my birthday. Being a whisker away from forty caused a cloud to pass, and gave me pause, making me stop and take stock on where I was and where I was going. That milestone—some say the entrance to middle age—is enough to make anyone think twice, or as Harold Raines says in *Flyfishing Through the Midlife Crisis,* the "black dog" is on our trail. But I know this: for me, a day spent welcoming spring under open skies is a way to reaffirm the joy of life, and preferable to any gift or party that others might desire. What can I say? Some men upon reaching this age buy a sports car, a few even take on a lover half their age, and here I am choosing rivers. But there's a method to this madness— rivers remind me of my younger seasons, remind me of endless days of summer freedom.

* * * *

The East Branch of the Swift River dances and sings, free like a child, coursing through hills toward the waiting Quabbin. Its dark grey-green waters are swollen from runoff, and white foam marks the many boulders in its path. I arrive just after dawn and the woods glisten, a fresh scent of evergreens wafting through the still air. A few patches of snow hold firm on north slopes, but the spring peepers announce the true season, and much of the snow will be gone by day's end.

Here at the Brooks Woodland Preserve, on the northeast side of the Quabbin, the river has about five miles to go as the crow flies to reach the reservoir, and probably twice that much on its twisting path. This was once the land of Nipmucks, and all that now remains to mark their presence are a group of boulders, once used as grinding stones. In the hollow of the boulders the natives pounded corn and acorns with stone pestles. The white settlers also made grist along the river, using the power of the water to turn the millstones which crushed the corn. Like the natives before them, they too left their mark in stone—miles and miles of stone walls crisscross the forest, and occasionally one comes upon an old cellar hole, a doorstep, or even a millstone.

Beneath pine and hardwoods I follow the river southward, past a marshy area, and into land owned by Harvard University called the Harvard Forest. It feels good to be on my feet, good to be on a trail I've never hiked before. The landscape is intimate, so crowded by trees and hills that I can only see a few feet ahead, making me wonder what's around the bend. New England is made for walking, and curiosity keeps you moving.

I veer off the trail, flush a wild turkey that runs rather than flies, and make my own path along the river. Ahead I can see the confluence where Moccasin Brook pours into the Swift at a right angle. The two currents collide, battling for supremacy, with the Moccasin boiling on top of the larger river before the union is complete.

A few minutes further downstream I turn to the east, this time stopping to admire a brook that cascades down a dark hillside. Enormous pines and hemlocks form a dense canopy, and there is little undergrowth except for mountain laurel and mayflower, almost ready to bloom. Rocks and trunks of trees have thick layers of green moss, almost florescent where a ray of sun has filtered through. I sit, scribbling my notes, resting my legs.

From my backpack I remove a book of quotations, and one of John Burrough's jumps out at me: "... To find the universal elements enough; to find the air and the water exhilarating, to be refreshed by a morning walk or an evening saunter ... to be thrilled by stars at night; to be elated over a bird's nest or a wild flower in the spring—these are some of the rewards of the simple life."

Then, a few pages later, a quote from Frank Lloyd Wright: " I believe in God, only I spell it Nature." Amen. I'm convinced nature gives us a glimpse into the perfect order of the divine.

I resume walking, following the river into the Swift River Reservation. A strange noise comes from the back of an open field. At first I think it a tree creaking in the wind, but there is no wind, and slowly I make my way toward the sound. I hear it again, and then I see it, a goshawk, perched on a branch looking at me, through me. It seems as if it means to stare me down, and it does; I stop short, the hair rising on the back of my neck.

Slowly I raise my binoculars and see its red eyes, as fierce a look as I've ever seen. It is obvious the hawk is about to attack, and I back away. That seems to satisfy the bird, and it flies into the woods, probably closer to the nest it must be guarding. Few birds, or any wild creature for that matter, protect its territory as aggressively as the goshawk.

Back along the river, the trail passes a broad marsh where the river fans out, and although I do not see a beaver dam, I suspect the marsh was originally created by beaver. Almost every stream anywhere near the Quabbin shows evidence of beaver, and its not unusual to see a new pond spring up where just a year earlier there was forest. One of the state's few environmental success stories, the beaver is making a strong comeback after being wiped out in Massachusetts by trapping over a century ago. The current population was reintroduced to the state by the Massachusetts Division of Fisheries and Wildlife.

Where the river tumbles out of the marsh, more ancient pines and hemlocks shade its dark waters, and trout suck up insects caught in the current. I revel in what is one of the best river walks I have ever been on, and figure I am about half way to the Quabbin. That's when I spot the KEEP OUT sign.

The thought that one person "owns" the next stretch of river by controlling the land around it, fouled my mood. My anger is not only directed at the owner, but also the reasons that caused him or her to post the property. Had idiots littered here? Threats of lawsuits? Whatever the reason, I turn back, find my way to the main road and hitch a ride to my car.

I glance at my map and decide to make a stop before resuming the river walk. I head to Petersham, with its lovely town green, and stop at the country store. Through the shelves of groceries I follow the scent of coffee to a room with low beamed ceiling and scattered tables. I pour myself a coffee, and order a sandwich and a piece of raspberry pie.

Refueled, I drive back to river, and park on Glen Valley Road, and resume my walk. I'm quite familiar with this part of the river from previous hikes and fishing trips, and at each pool I remember the people I came with. There was one trip with my brother Mark that is especially clear, because the conversation began with the river and turned into much more. It started when I made a sweeping gesture of the river with my hands and said "This is how I picture heaven."

Mark thought about that, nodded, and said "I think we keep coming back until we get it right. That's why some people are at such a higher level of understanding than others; they have been here many times."

We talked of rivers, life and the afterlife, as only brothers can.

Now I continue downstream, thinking of coming back until I get it right, thinking I'll be coming back often. The memory of our conversation seems to merge with the present, and I maintain the thought process as if Mark were walking with me. A picture flashes through my mind of the two of us as young boys, rambling home from a day of fishing. Certain places have the power to connect the past to the present, as if time between them is no more than a blink.

Where the river crosses Route 32A, on its final leg to Quabbin, I notice pellets of scat piled high outside a culvert. Porcupine. I chuckle, thinking of another odd place a porcupine had made its den—my cabin's outhouse. Being a true "flatlander" when I first bought the place, I had no idea what those pellets were which spilled from the sides of the outhouse. It's only by the grace of God I didn't get a butt full of quills.

Porcupines also made me think of Paul Rezendes, a professional wildlife tracker, who knows the Quabbin like the back of his hand. I once interviewed him about his book, *Tracking and the Art of Seeing*. Our conversation was conducted while walking through the woods, and Paul soon picked up the trail of a porcupine, so we followed, forgetting all about the interview, absorbed in reading the signs on the forest floor.

It's funny what you remember about a person or day in the woods. I recall being surprised when Paul casually explained that at one time he was an avid hunter. He explained that the more his skills increased the closer he got to the animals, and finally he decided he could not kill any more.

"The more time I spend in the woods," he said softly, "the more I realize everything is connected. What's happening out in the forest is also happening to me."

Now, as I follow the Swift River's final mile to Quabbin, I think of being connected. Am I? As soon as you think about it, the connection slips. For me, that special feeling comes in snatches, usually when I'm walking in the woods and realize I'm not thinking of anything, just letting my body lead. The pure joy of moving puts away the mind's cluttered thoughts and I become one with the forest. I believe these few minutes are my own fountain of youth, a therapeutic time when my mind's propensity to analyze shuts down, and true peace spreads through me.

The river slows considerably as it approaches Potapoag Pond, a finger-like extension of the main body of Quabbin.

When fishing this stretch I never know if it's a pickerel or a trout fighting at the end of the line. Potapoag is loaded with warm-water species, such as pickerel and sunfish, and I suspect a number of large granddaddy bass sit back a bit from the mouth of the Swift and wait for dinner to come riding on the current.

Near the mouth of the river, I sit, lean back against the hill and let the sun strike my face. It would be so easy to take a catnap here, to let Quabbin's serenity wash over me the way it calms the Swift. I've followed the river to its end but there's still one more thing I need to see. I hike over a ridge and find my way to one of the old roads inside the reservoir's boundaries, near gate 40. Rather than walk toward my car, I follow the road a mile into the forest until it forks around a grassy opening. Surrounding the triangular green are a multitude of cellar holes covered with moss, leaves and vines.

This was once the center of Dana; now it is a ghost town.

I stand quietly at the fork until a woodpecker's drumming floats from the forest, interrupting the thick silence. Poking around the edge of the green, I examine cellar holes and stone walls, and listen for voices from the past. Trees grow from some of the cellar holes, but the stonework looks as snug as the day it was built. On the south side of the green a large maple has an opening in its side, big enough for me to step into, like a casket standing on its end. For a moment I am ten years old again, remembering a book Mark and I read about a boy who lived for a year in a hollow tree.

Dusk is falling. Sitting in the center of the green I visualize the homes that once faced inward, and see soft light shining

from the windows. Inside one home I see women gathered together at a husking bee, gabbing and smiling, enjoying the gos-
sip that makes the work seem less tiresome. From the darkening
woods I see men returning from the fields, and far down the
hill, from the direction of the Swift River, I see two barefoot
boys running, fishing poles on their shoulders. They look like
brothers.

EXPLORER'S NOTES

Recommended reading

Quabbin: The Accidental Wilderness by Thomas Conuel.
An Atlas of the Quabbin Valley, Past and Present by J. R. Greene.

Notes on the Quabbin

Information and historic exhibits are at the Quabbin Visitors
  Center, just off Route 9 (413-323-7221).
The Trustees of Reservations own a number of properties in the
  greater Petersham area (508-921-1944).

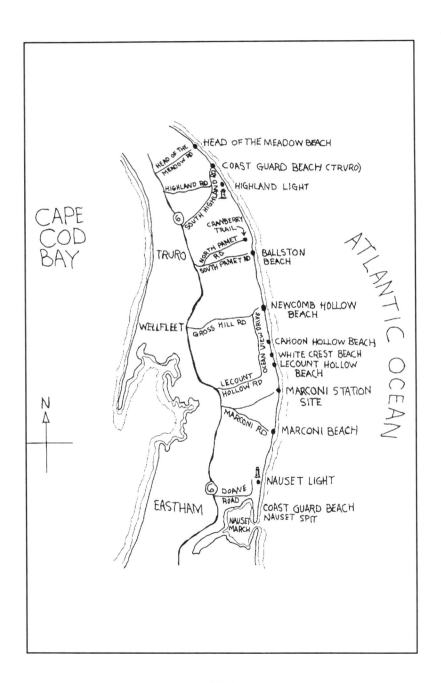

Solitude— Cape Cod National Seashore in Winter

Along the water's edge, no more than ten feet into the surf, a seal cruises, heading in the same direction I am walking. For a short distance we are side by side, sharing the harsh world of the beach in winter.

Except for gulls, the seal is the only other living thing I can see. The summer crowds are gone, and the bright multicolored blankets, umbrellas and bathing suits are replaced by miles of uninterrupted shore in austere patterns of brown sand and white snow. Earlier, when I started the walk, it was almost all white, with snow falling almost horizontally in a short but furious burst. The flakes quickly changed to tiny pellets, not really sleet, but looking and feeling more like bits of Styrofoam used in packing. When the snow stopped, and visibility increased, I could see slate grey sky, the same color as the ocean. The Atlantic was dark and forboding, and on the horizon it was difficult to discern where the ocean ended and the sky began.

When one thinks of New England frontiers, the Northern Forest usually comes to mind, or perhaps remote pockets in the Berkshires. But this long, thin sliver of sand on the forearm of Cape Cod is a frontier in its own right, a strange desert on the edge of the sea. Nature has her way here, using wind and water to tear away one place and create a new one. Dunes are formed, sandbars breached, and human structures are sometimes torn away by an angry Atlantic.

Walking the beach in winter is entirely different than hiking inland, not just because of the ocean environment, but also because of the feeling of spaciousness. With no obstacles, no trees or rocks, just the flat expanse of shore, your legs can be on automatic pilot, your eyes seeing but not really seeing. I've walked for ten minutes or more on the beach with my thoughts miles away, something I'm unable to do most other places. In many ways a seaside outing is a lonely affair, an adventure in solitude. And that's the beauty of it.

Would I still relish the sense of space and the severity of the shoreline if I were here for more than a two-day tramp? Would I continue to see starkness as beauty? Henry Beston did. He lived on Nauset Spit for a year, beginning in 1927, and never did his sense of joy and wonder fade. His classic book, *The Outermost House,* chronicles the natural world of dunes, shore, marsh and sea.

Having just re-read his book, I feel something of Beston's spirit with me as I walk Nauset Spit (also known as Coast Guard Beach). My eye seems a bit sharper, picking up subtleties I might otherwise miss. The curl of the waves, the snow on beach grass, and the golden hues of the marsh all seem more vivid. Even sounds seem more distinct. At first, all I heard was the constant roar of the ocean, but in time the ear discerns other patterns, such as the clacking, grinding sound of a receding wave rolling over pebbles.

After a half hour of walking south from the Coast Guard Beach parking area, I rest a moment at the approximate site of Beston's simple two-room cottage, called the "Fo'castle." It's gone now, having been swept out to sea by surging storm tides during the blizzard of 1978. But the essence of the place is the same: wild, lonely and seemingly barren. Just beyond the breakers, however, I can, with the aid of binoculars, see bird activity. One bird, which appears to be a red-breasted merganser, keeps diving beneath the waves, finally emerging with a fish. Immediately a gull swoops down to steal the catch, but the merganser is quicker, slipping under the surface with the fish still in its mouth. Farther out, buffleheads bob on swells, and farther out still is a single loon, its pale brown plumage so different than the vivid black-and-white pattern of summer. Beston was right about the winter when he wrote, "My beach is empty, but not the ocean beyond."

I put the binoculars back in my pack and continue the short distance to Nauset Inlet, hoping to find seals. The inlet connects the ocean to Nauset Marsh. Sand eels use the marsh as a nursery, and seals come to feed on the eels and sun themselves on the shoals that emerge at low tide. But today the seals are nowhere to be seen, apparently off at another preferred feeding and resting location.

Seals were not always welcomed on the Cape. During the late nineteenth and much of the twentieth century there was a bounty on seals, and fishermen would kill them, fearing that they were eating too many fish. But it was humans who were driving the fish stocks down by overfishing, while the seals were feeding primarily on sandlance, a small fish with virtually no commercial value. The killing of seals was finally halted in 1972 with the passage of the Marine Mammal Protection Act, and today there are a few thousand seals wintering along the Cape.

From the tip of Nauset Spit there is a good view of the marsh it protects. Striped bass, scallops, flounder, quahogs and other marine species all make use of the marsh. When Beston lived here, the dunes that protect the marsh from the sea were much higher. But the storm that obliterated Beston's cottage sent waves sweeping over the dunes, reducing them to small mounds. Another big storm might finish the job, re-creating the Cape once again.

The most dramatic evidence of the forces of change on the Cape is just to the south of Coast Guard Beach in the town of Chatham. Here the Atlantic has broken through the narrow strip of sand known as Nauset Beach (called North Beach by the locals), which once extended for eleven miles, serving as a buffer against the open ocean. In 1987 a nor'easter, combined with unusually high tides, created a breach in the barrier beach at its narrowest point, and within a week the opening was almost a quarter mile wide. Within five years the cut had expanded to two miles, and the Atlantic was free to pound what was once the inner shore. Land eroded and homes toppled into the sea. Yet the break was not wholly unexpected. Nauset Beach had been moving between five and ten feet per year, getting narrower and longer in the process. As the sands shifted, the barrier beach was weakened. The break that came was predicted by a few locals who knew both history and geology. Breaks had occurred in 1740, 1851 and 1871.

The ocean takes what she gives, and the true rulers of the Cape are surf and wind.

* * * *

As I leave the inlet and head back north along the shore, the sun breaks through the clouds. It's late afternoon, and I can see the top of Nauset Lighthouse, illuminated by the sun. Its red beacon flashes, drawing me like a magnet, and I decide to walk the shoreline to it, knowing it's probably the last time I will see it in this particular spot. Resting at the very edge of the cliff, the 250-ton 48-foot-tall lighthouse is in danger of collapsing into the ocean, as erosion continues its steady advance. But like the smaller lighthouses built on skids, Nauset Light will be moved inland by giant machinery, and a piece of the Cape's history will be saved.

How ironic, that the lighthouse which saved so many sailors from the sea is now threatened. This back side of the Cape has been the graveyard of more than 3,000 ships, and the toll would have been much higher were it not for the lighthouses and the organized rescue teams. In 1786 the Massachusetts Humane Society was established to provide shelter huts along the coast for shipwreck survivors, and lifeboat stations where surfboats and line-throwing guns could be stored for the use of volunteer crews. In 1871 the U. S. Congress appropriated money for the construction and manning of nine stations on the back side of the Cape to be manned by professionals of the Life Saving Service, which later became the Coast Guard.

Beston witnessed several wrecks during his winter here, none so sad as the plight of the *Montclair*, a three-masted schooner carrying lathes, which broke apart in tremendous seas:

"Seven men clung to the rocking, drifting mass that was once the stern. Dragging over the shoal ground, the mass rocked on its keel, now rolling the men sickeningly high, now tumbling them down into the trampling rush of seas. Five clung to the skylight of the afterdeck house, two to the stern-rail balustrade. One great sea wall drowned all the five. Men on the beach saw it coming and shouted, the men on the deck-house shouted and were heard, and then the wave broke, hiding the tragic fragment in a sluice of foam and wreckage. When this had poured away the men on the afterhouse were gone."

Amazingly the other two sailors, one a boy of seventeen and the other a stockily built man, survived:

"The wave tore the boy from the balustrade, but the stocky man reached out, caught him, and held on. The tide rising, the stern began to approach the beach. A detail of men hurriedly sent over from Nauset Station now appeared on the beach and managed to reach and rescue the survivors."

Beston goes on to describe that even as the vessel was breaking up, "men came to the beach and helped themselves to the lathes and what wreckage they fancied." He adds that a week later a local man was walking the shore and came upon a hand thrust up from the sands, and buried beneath was the body of a crew member from the *Montclair*.

* * * *

The walk north along the shore toward the lighthouse has an altogether different feel than the walk to the inlet. Here I felt trapped by the enormous cliffs of sand and gravel on my left and the pounding surf on my right. Only a narrow strip of beach separated ocean from the bluff. The sound of the waves was more menacing here and I wondered if it was caused by the cliffs, or simply my imagination. Clay crumbled from sections of the glacial scarps, and the color of sand ranged from light tan near the cliff top to a dark chocolate hue at the bottom. The massive trunk of a pine tree lay across the beach and I wondered if it had floated here all the way from Maine.

The cliff blocked the sun from the beach and a mist was trapped in the shadows ahead. When I turned and looked back at Coast Guard Beach, which was still bathed in light, it was like looking through a dark tunnel to the land of the sun. Late afternoon light is the most beautiful of a winter's day, and where the sun illuminated the breakers it had a soft, violet tinge.

I made my mistake when the lighthouse came into view again. The setting sun lit the top of the beacon, making for an incredible contrast to the dark beach below. I stopped to take pictures, waiting a few minutes between each shot for the changing scene caused by the sinking of the sun. Where the sea met the sky was a dark strip of gray, then just above a band of pink, followed by blue-black sky. While I was looking for just the right shot a wave came in and washed over my feet, making me jump to the base of the cliff. Looking south toward the parking lot, I realized the tide had been rising, and now there was only a couple feet of exposed sand.

Throwing my camera into my pack I raced back along the beach. Twice, a wave washed high, forcing me to literally hug the cliff to keep from getting wet. When I passed the pine log and the clay mound, I slowed to a trot as the dry section of beach was now four feet wide. If one big wave had knocked my feet out from under me, my little walk on the beach could have been a disaster. I could just see the headlines; "Idiot writer succumbs while trapped at Nauset." From now on I'd pay more attention to tides before being mesmerized by light, shadows and colors.

* * * *

I'm beginning to believe that there is no such thing as coincidence. After running off the beach I headed directly to The Over Look Inn where I had made reservations for the night's lodging. Innkeepers Ian and Nan Aitchison met me at the door, and I explained I had just come from Nauset Spit, retracing Henry Beston's daily walks. They broke into big smiles, and Nan said, "Then we must put you in the room Beston used when he slept here."

"Beston slept here?" I asked.

Ian nodded, and explained how Beston would occasionally leave the Fo'castle and spend the night at the inn when he wanted companionship and comfort. At that time the land around The Over Look Inn was devoid of trees, and Beston could actually see the inn from the beach. When Beston needed supplies or wanted to stay at the inn, he would wave a lantern at a preset time and Mr. or Mrs. Kelley, who owned the inn during Beston's time, would then pick him up in their Model-T Ford the next day.

Ian laughed and said, "This was during Prohibition and some of the townfolks thought that Mr. Kelley and Beston were in the rum-running business, thinking the lantern signals meant a shipment of contraband had arrived."

Nan excused herself and returned with a first edition of *The Outermost House*. In the forward Beston had written:

"I would close with the acknowledgement of a special and very great obligation, my debt to Mr. and Mrs. Thomas Kelley of The Over Look Inn in Eastham. Without their constant and ever-thoughtful aid, without their hospitable roof to turn to on occasion, without their friendly care of my interests ashore it would have been perhaps impossible to remain upon the beach. With heartfelt gratitude do I thank them here. Long may their hospitable doors stand open on Cape Cod!"

Beston, like Thoreau, knew the dangers of living alone, writing that "in utter solitude odd things may happen to the mind ... . I made no pretense acting the conventional hermit." He regularly went into town, visited The Over Look, and walked the beach with Coast Guard patrols.

"It was not this touch with my fellows, however, that alone sustained me. Dwelling thus upon the dunes, I lived in the midst of an abundance of natural life which manifested itself every hour of the day, and from being thus surrounded, thus enclosed within a great whirl of what one may call the life force, I felt that I drew a secret and sustaining energy."

* * * *

The Over Look Inn has a rare character and charm, and so do its owners. The moment you walk in the door you have a feeling of things solid, of things permanent and of things functional and elegant. It is a home where history is loved. Old photos adorn the walls, every manner of history book fills the many bookcases, and the rooms have brass beds and claw-foot tubs.

By the doorway is a set of deer antlers with hats hanging, and nearby are a wide array of walking staffs.

The inn dates back to 1869, and sits on a hill across from the marshes of Coast Guard Beach. It was built by Captain Barnabus Chipman as a wedding gift to his wife. The Aitchisons have put their touch on the Victorian mansion with the Ernest Hemingway Billiard Room and the Winston Churchill Library, which is where I spent a pleasant evening by the fire talking to my hosts and reading more of *The Outermost House.*

I described my day at Coast Guard Beach to Ian, which prompted him to comment, "What changes to that land I've seen! The Coast Guard spit was much wider and higher with big dunes not too long ago. Won't be surprised if the ocean rolls right over it all and it becomes a sand bar. When that happens I'm afraid some of the homes around the marsh could be threatened."

Listening to Ian I thought of how Beston's house was washed away by the sea. Perhaps it was a fitting end to have it go by nature's hand, at nature's time. There was a picture of Beston's beloved Fo'castle in the book Nan had let me read, and it really was a handsome little cottage. Compact, lined with windows, and featuring a small porch facing the sea, it looked like the perfect writer's retreat. As the fire crackled, I daydreamed of how wonderful it would be to take a year off from the routine of civilization and live within the cycle of nature.

* * * *

The next day I returned to the beach, only this time farther out on the Cape's forearm, in Truro at Ballston Beach. The sky was crystal blue, temperatures in the forties, and only a light breeze came in off the rolling breakers. A perfect day to combat cabin fever and quench a thirst for sunlight. Unlike the day before, I timed my walk with the low tide, so that there would be no chance of getting stranded.

I had the shore to myself and headed northward, first following the beach, then a path that led away from the ocean into hills covered with scrub pine. With nothing to give the scrawny trees scale, the hills looked like Vermont's green mountains rolling off in the distance. Before the white man came, much of the Cape was covered with forest. But the timber disappeared, first for farmland and firewood, later for shipbuilding, housing and charcoal.

Thoreau visited the Cape in the 1850s at a time when most of the peninsula had been stripped of its trees, and even the topsoil was blowing away. He was fascinated by the barren and dramatic scenery around him, so different than the fields and woodlands of Concord. He called the outer Cape "as wild and solitary as the Western prairies used to be" and compared his trip through it as "traveling a desert." Yet still he knew the Cape's lure and prophetically wrote, "The time must come when this coast will be a place of resort for those New-Englanders who really wish to visit the sea-side. But this shore will never be more attractive than it is now."

Thoreau hated traveling through settled areas, and in his book *Cape Cod,* he sticks primarily to the coast, walking from the Eastham area to Provincetown, a landlubber fascinated by the power of the sea. His journey has its moments of humor, as well. Finding a six-inch sea-clam on the beach, he "carried it along, thinking to try an experiment." Cooking the clam on the embers of a small fire he kindled on the beach, he ate it, finding it sweet and savory, yet also rather tough. Later that evening, while lodging at the house of a Wellfleet oysterman, he began "to feel the potency of the clam" and "was made quite sick by it" while his host laughed at his expense. Thoreau too found humor in his illness, observing that when the Pilgrims first landed on Cape Cod they became sick from clams, and his experience was a "valuable confirmation of their story, and I am prepared now to believe every word of Mourt's Relation." His wit was just as sharp for the women he met while on the Cape:

"A strict regard for truth obliges us to say that the few women whom we saw that day looked exceedingly pinched up. They had prominent chins and noses, having lost all their teeth, and a sharp W would represent their profile. A Nauset woman, of hardness and coarseness such as no man ever possesses or suggests. It was enough to see the vertebrae and sinews of her neck, and her set jaws of iron, which would have bitten a board-nail in two in their ordinary actions ... who looked as if it made her head ache to live."

I had Thoreau's book with me, and when the path crested the top of the cliff, I sat and read, occasionally stopping to look below. Row upon row of breakers sparkled in the sun, and the dune was so high I had traded places with the birds, looking down at two gulls sailing by. As far as the eye could see the beach was empty—amazing, considering that such solitude can be found within a day's drive from one-quarter of the nation's population.

Of course, without the protection of the National Seashore, there would probably be a home within a stone's throw of my lofty perch. The creation of the park in 1961 wasn't easy, especially since there were 600 homes within its proposed borders. Much of the credit for the park's creation must go to John F. Kennedy, who had seen commercialism spread across his beloved Cape Cod, and he became a vocal proponent of the park. He, along with other park advocates, crafted a bill that allowed homes within the proposed boundaries to remain in private ownership, an important provision for securing Congressional approval. Today the National Seashore encompasses 43,000 acres, a patchwork of federal, local and private ownership.

When I resumed my walk, the path led through beach heather, bayberry, and more stunted pines before leading down to the shore. At first glance a beach walk might seem dull, with nothing to break the monotony of blue ocean and tawny sand. But soon the eye discerns the little things, like the mosaic of clay I saw in the cliffs. In one spot I marveled at a mixture of sand and clay that had poured off the cliff like a probing finger of lava, freezing solid over snow at the base of the cliff. Near the water's edge were pebbles of all colors, worn smooth by the waves and twinkling under the winter sun.

When Thoreau sauntered over this very same stretch of shore, he too found pebbles a source of fascination, filling his pockets with the best specimens, only to cull the collection when the stones dried and were not so brilliant. He examined driftwood that lay twisted about the beach, noting that many of the locals collected their fuel and lumber from wood washed up on the beach. At various intervals he watched townsfolk scavenge the waterline for useful items washed ashore from the wrecks that littered the ocean's floor just off shore. "There is no telling what it [the sea] may vomit up," he wrote. "It is still heaving up the tow-cloth of the Franklin, and perhaps a piece of some old pirate's ship."

But for Thoreau, as well as most of us who venture out to the spine of the Cape, it's the sea that captures the eye. And just now a wind was coming over the hundred-foot dunes, hitting the top of the waves at the curl, the wind lifting off a film of spray, flinging it skyward. I must have walked another couple miles daydreaming, just staring at the play of the surf and the changing hues of ocean colors. The sea is a wilderness; beautiful, powerful and frightening. Come in winter, walk for hours and let it energize you.

EXPLORER'S NOTES

Recommended reading

Cape Cod, by Henry David Thoreau, Princeton University Press. Edition recommended for its comprehensive index.

A Journal of the Pilgrims at Plymouth—Mourt's Relation, Corinth Books. An anonymous first-hand account of the Pilgrims' journey to the new world, including their exploration of Cape Cod before they settled in Plymouth.

The Outermost House, by Henry Beston. A must-read for nature lovers.

Other walks

While my favorite walk is along the shoreline of the National Seashore, the park also has several self-guiding nature trails that allow for easier walking. The Fort Hill Trail, about a mile and half long, crosses open fields and offers wonderful vistas of Nauset Marsh (located on Governor Prence Road in Eastham). The Red Maple Swamp Trail is adjacent to Fort Hill, and features boardwalk sections through a red maple swamp. The one-mile Nauset Marsh Trail runs from Salt Pond Visitor Center, passing through fields and forest and alongside Salt Pond and Nauset Marsh.

In Wellfleet, I'm partial to the Atlantic White Cedar Trail, which takes about an hour to walk. It's located in Wellfleet near the Marconi Station area. The National Seashore's longest trail is the is the three-mile walk to Jeremy Point at Great Island. At high tide the last portion of the trail is underwater, so time your walk accordingly. It's located on Chequesset Neck Road on the bay side of Wellfleet. The Pilgrim Spring Trail will take you by the spring where the Pilgrims may have drunk their first New England water. The three-fourths-mile-long trail is located at the Pilgrim Heights Area of Truro. In Provincetown, try the Beech Forest Trail, where the mile-long trail passes through a unique region where dunes and beech trees jockey for dominance. It's located on Race Point Road.

Trail tips

Be sure to stay on the trails and do not step on dune grass. The extensive root system of the grass holds the dunes together.

Salt Pond Visitor Center

First-time visitors to the Cape should stop in at the Salt Pond Visitor Center on Route 6 in Eastham. It features a variety of natural-history resources, maps, orientation movies, a museum, and knowledgeable park rangers. You might also want to purchase a video sold in area bookstores, produced by SITE Productions and entitled *Cape Cod and the Islands.*

Advice on camping

Camping is not permitted within the National Seashore except at the designated privately-operated campgrounds listed here:
Horton's Park, North Truro (508-487-1220).
North of Highland, North Truro (508-487-1191).
North Truro Camping Area, North Truro (508-487-1847).
Nickerson State Forest, a state-owned campground located nearby (508-896-3491).

Selected accommodations

The Overlook Inn (508-255-1886).
Cape Cod Chamber of Commerce (508-362-3225).

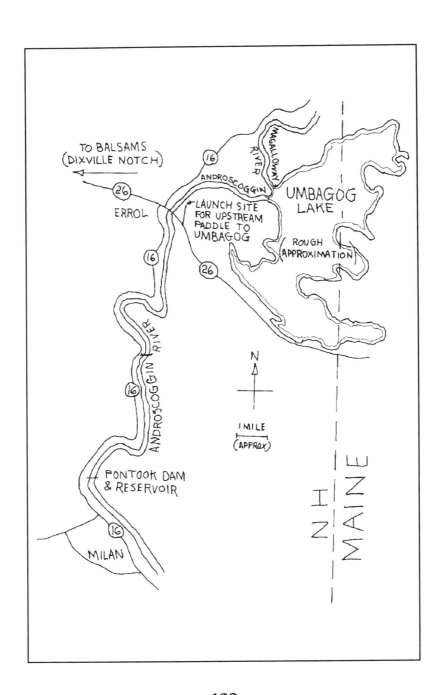

TO BALSAMS
(DIXVILLE NOTCH)

16

MAGALLOWAY RIVER

UMBAGOG LAKE

26

ERROL

ANDROSCOGGIN

LAUNCH SITE
FOR UPSTREAM
PADDLE TO
UMBAGOG

16

26

ROUGH
APPROXIMATION

N

1 MILE
(APPROX)

ANDROSCOGGIN RIVER

16

PONTOOK DAM
& RESERVOIR

16

MILAN

N H

MAINE

Lake Umbagog and the Androscoggin River

I'd never gone trout fishing with a guide before, so I jumped at the chance when my friend Ed invited me to join him on a drift boat with guide Jon Howe. I was even more happy about my decision when we arrived at the upper reaches of the Androscoggin River in New Hampshire. The river was running high, with dark waves rolling over submerged boulders—not the kind of water to fish from a canoe. Nor did it look like wading would be easy; the Androscoggin is wide, deep and swift. (I later learned that the river was running unusually high for summer. In a more typical year the section below the Mollidgewock Campground is enjoyed by canoeists who can handle class I-II whitewater.)

We launched just below the village of Errol at dawn, and I quickly realized just how well suited a drift boat is for this river. Waves that would terrify me in a canoe were handled with ease by Howe, and the drift boat gently glided over them. The boat was so steady, in fact, that we could stand in the bow and cast while bobbing through rapids.

Another pleasant realization was that Howe fit my idea of what a good guide should be. He obviously knew the river, the fish, and the art of fly fishing, but it was the way he shared his knowledge that made the float so enjoyable. Rather than overpower us with advice or instructions, Howe sprinkled his tips at intervals, letting the beauty of the river be the focal point of the trip rather than himself. I asked him how he got into the business, and he explained that as a kid he would go on camping trips with his family in the Rockies, learning to fly fish at a young age. Later, he followed his passion to be outdoors, becoming a land surveyor, fly-fishing instructor and guide. Today he was clearly enjoying himself, working the oars to keep us on course and occasionally dropping anchor at a choice location.

"Don't pass up any water," offered Howe, "we've caught nice fish in the middle of rapids as well as quiet eddies." And so Ed and I took turns casting from the bow into all kinds of water. Our first fish was a small Atlantic salmon that cleared the water like a rocket, and surprised me with its strength. Then came a brookie from a shaded pool near shore, followed by a nice-sized rainbow taken from whitewater. Minutes later a brown trout, that was holding just behind an island, hit Ed's Alder fly imitation. I looked at my watch: we had been on the river half an hour and had caught four species of game fish.

I asked Howe if this was common. "Every trip is different, but we almost always catch fish. Usually they range in size like they have today, from ten to thirteen inches, but every now and then someone hooks into something more substantial. Last year we landed an eighteen-inch brook trout and a six-pound brown in the same week. We release all the fish we catch to keep the fishing first-rate."

The size of the brook trout surprised me, but not the brown. A biologist at the New Hampshire Fish and Game Department had told me about the Androscoggin's legendary browns. He explained that the browns can tolerate warm water better than the other species, and that when the river warms up in July and August they hide in deep holes by day, then venture out on nocturnal forays. Some of the holes in the river are over thirty feet deep, and occasionally a lucky angler who drifts a fly near the bottom feels the jarring tug of an Androscoggin brown.

As our boat bobbed along, I settled back and enjoyed the ride. The river flows due south here, through an area known as Thirteen Mile Wilderness, before turning east at the town of Gorham and heading into Maine. On our left was a jagged ridge of spruce and fir, while to the right Route 16 parallels the river. There are no homes or stores to mar the scenery. I knew there were plenty of moose nearby, because that morning we saw a cow and calf cross Route 16 near our launch site.

The Androscoggin is one of New England's major waterways, rising in Lake Umbagog and flowing 167 miles to the Atlantic through Maine's Merrymeeting Bay. The case could be made that the true river is much longer, and that the Magalloway River and Androscoggin are actually one long river. If you look on a map you will see that the Magalloway River flows into Lake Umbagog at a spot quite close to where the Androscoggin leaves the lake. Page Helm Jones, author of *The Evolution of a Valley, the Androscoggin Story*, discusses the issue, writing, "The sources of all our rivers have been controversial, but doubly so when used in determining international or even state boundaries. The little known Androscoggin River is no exception even though the name of the river does not appear in the controversy. The reason for this is that the Androscoggin is not called by that name until the junction of the Magalloway River and the outlet from Umbagog Lake at Errol, New Hampshire. Prior to that point, it is called the Magalloway River. This dates back to Indian times when there were no fewer than seven sections of the river which bore distinct names."

Whatever its true length, this upper stretch of the river is a true gem. Farther downstream, where the river turns toward Maine, the Androscoggin is still cleansing itself of the dioxin released into the river by the paper mills. (Dioxin is a byproduct of the chlorine used to bleach paper.) Progress is being made in the fight against pollution, such as a recent pact in Maine to reduce the discharge of dioxin to the point where fish in the river will be safe to eat in four years. More immediate progress is evidenced by the announcement that the fifteen-mile stretch of river from the New Hampshire state line to Sunday River is now deemed swimmable. Even the pristine upper stretch where we were floating had its problems from the logging industry.

"At certain times of the year it was impossible to see the surface of the water as thousand of cords of pulpwood stretched for miles from bank to bank," writes Jones. "From time to time log booms strung across the river on steel cables separated stretches of water above the rapids so that pulpwood could be released as needed at the mills downstream at Berlin."

It's hard to imagine this stretch of water being anything but the way it is now: beautiful and wild. And there are more rivers to the north that are just like it, offering the explorer a lifetime of weekend trips of fishing and canoeing. Louise Dickenson

Rich sang their virtues and those of the surrounding lakes in her 1942 book, *We Took to the Woods:*

"Kennebago to Rangeley to Cupsuptic down they drop, level to level, through short snarling rivers: Mooselukmeguntic to the Richardsons to Pond-in-the-River, and through Rapid River to Umbagog, whence they empty into the Androscoggin and begin the long south-easterly curve back to the ocean. I like to say their names, and I wish I could make you see them— long, lovely, lonely stretches of water shut in by dark hills."

* * * *

Morning stretches into noon as we roll down the river, landing small fish but not the lunker browns that rule the depths. Stretches of fast water and smooth glides run one after the other, and the only sound is the low murmur of the river itself. A great blue heron rises from the shore and lazily flaps its way down river. We follow, Jon pulling on the oars primarily for steering, rocking over rapids and drifting like a fallen leaf through the flat water. Soon we begin to catch smallmouth bass, which put up a mighty fight, bulldogging down to the depths, then breaking the surface in an effort to free the hook. Like the trout, we catch them in all kinds of water, but the bigger ones come when we drift muddler minnows into deep pools.

After lunch we fish a little more, but the sun has put the trout down, and our casts are half-hearted. But the river entertains us with its waves, colors and motion, and I feel like following it to the sea. Some day ... .

That night, long after I'm off the water, when I'm just about to drift off to sleep, I still feel like I'm in the boat, gently rising and falling over waves. I replay the fight of a rainbow, see the spruce and fir roll by, and imagine I can smell that wonderful river scent of flowing water. A river can stay with you along time. As the poet and novelist James Dickey wrote:

"The river and everything I remembered about it became a possession to me, a personal, private possession, as nothing else in my life ever had. Now it ran nowhere but in my head, but there it ran as though immortality ... . In me it still is, and will be until I die, green, rocky, deep, fast, slow, and beautiful beyond reality."

* * * *

When you visit the northeast corner of New Hampshire, you basically have two choices when night falls. You can camp out, at such a fine site as the Mollidgewock Campground along the Androscoggin, or you can go to the other extreme and stay at one of New England's grand old resorts, the Balsams. Ed and I chose the Balsams, and after a couple days on the river and tramping through the woods, enjoyed total luxury.

Located in Dixville Notch on Route 26, the Balsams suddenly appears around a bend in the road, majestic and breathtaking, like a castle in the wilderness. It's an extraordinary place, a throw-back to yesteryear when America offered diversity in its hotels and restaurants, before the chains made our choices homogeneous, bland and boring. When you stay at the Balsams you don't forget your visit. Maybe its the magnificent setting in the notch, with towering mountains rising on all sides, or maybe it's the hotel itself, looking like a resort in the Swiss Alps, with service that pays attention to your every need. Whatever the reason, the Balsams could be the perfect destination getaway for a "wild places" lover to share a weekend with a "comfort" lover. If one partner wants to spend all day hiking or fishing, the other can golf or lounge by the pool, and both can do so right at the Balsams. It might be stretching a little to say marriages can be saved by spending a weekend at the Balsams, but then again maybe not. It's truly one of the few places where both can find what each is looking for.

The Balsams is really a self-contained village, with services such as baby-sitting, church sermons, movies in a 250-seat theater, a beauty shop and barbershop. For the sports enthusiast there is golf, tennis, hiking trails, alpine and cross-country skiing in the winter, and mountain biking. Ed and I enjoyed what was right outside our door, a large swimming pool overlooking Lake Gloriette and the towering cliffs of the notch. And if the Androscoggin had not been so productive, we could have fly-fished in the stocked waters of Lake Gloriette from the rowboats available to guests.

From the pool I gazed to the east, watching clouds sail over the mountains shading the jagged notch. Over 15,000 acres are owned by the Balsams, almost all of it rugged, forested mountains. Peregrine falcons, a rare streamlined hawk that can fly like a bullet, nest in the exposed cliffs, swooping down on unsuspecting birds for its meals. Other rare creatures may live here too, perhaps even the mountain lion. It once roamed New England, but the white settlers put a bounty on its head, hunting and poisoning it to the point where it was extirpated from the region by the late 1800s.

I floated on my back and watched the light play over the mountains, clouds casting shadows that made the forest appear almost black. From such a distance the trees themselves appear to be a single species of conifer, but if you climb these hills you discover a wide mix of hardwoods and softwoods, tending to segregate themselves by elevations. In the lowlands, balsam fir, white cedar and the graceful tamarack (which sheds its needles) grow along backwoods swamps. Spruce and hemlocks are scattered among the hardwoods in the higher ground, giving way to red spruce, and then black spruce, and finally hardy balsam fir just before the treeline.

Hemlocks, tamaracks and cedars are fairly easy to identify. Seen from a car or an open area, the balsam fir has a compact crown that tapers to a point, while the spruce is looser and broader, but it can be difficult to distinguish spruce from fir deep in a forest. Whenever I drive to the north country from my home in southern New England, I try to look for the "north woods line," where the oaks and white pines begin to give way to the spruce and fir, as if giving the traveler an official welcome to the wilder country of moose, fisher and bobcat.

* * * *

The Androscoggin again entertained Ed and me on our second day of exploration, only this time instead of floating the rapids downstream, we used the river as our upstream route to one of New Hampshire's wildest lakes. Straddling the Maine-New Hampshire border, Lake Umbagog beckons the explorer with fifty miles of wild shoreline. We had no illusions about exploring it all in a weekend trip, so we set our sights on something we had never seen before—a nesting bald eagle.

With the aid of an electric motor mounted on the back of our canoe, we made good time covering the three miles of the

Androscoggin River that ran between our launch site, just off Route 26, and the lake. (One could launch directly into Lake Umbagog, but there's something adventurous about entering a lake from a river. It's also the quicker way to see the eagle's nest situated near where the Androscoggin exits the lake.) On our way upstream we made frequent stops, poking into backwater sloughs where we scared up a common merganser, a female with crested brown head and pure white throat. A handsome bird, large and sleek, and as adept at chasing down fish as a loon. Other birds—a wood duck, a ring-necked duck, a night heron and two great blue herons—took flight as we explored the maze of channels.

Back on the river, we trolled two lines behind the boat, but evidently there are few fish in this stretch or the mergansers had got to them first. Even though the current was slow, brisk gusts of wind swirled about the river, so the motor came in handy. With the motor angled to one side, we were able to paddle on the other, doubling our speed across the final mile to the lake. Then with the lake in sight, framed by blue-green mountains, we cut the motor and paddled the rest of the way. I was glad we did, because we were greeted by the mournful wail of a loon, then minutes later by the screech of an osprey.

The lake is a big one, sprawling some 7,800 acres in a generally north–south direction, with plenty of islands and coves for exploring. Its waters, however, are relatively shallow. Yellow perch, smallmouth bass, and lake chub are scattered throughout the lake, with salmon, brook trout and browns in the northern section, where there are some deep holes. The lake even has a floating island (held together by roots of grasses, shrubwood and bushes) that changes locations in the marshy area near where the Androscoggin leaves Umbagog.

Surrounding the lake is some of the most diverse habitat in New England: flood-plain forests of silver maple, red maple and elm, swamps with uncommon white cedar, and bogs filled with sphagnum moss, Labrador tea, tamarack, and carnivorous pitcher plants. Along rockier parts of the lake shore are jack pines, a relatively rare tree in New Hampshire and Maine. Thankfully much of the shoreline is protected within the Lake Umbagog National Wildlife Refuge, a mixture of private and public lands established in 1992. As wild as the shoreline is, it's still easily accessible to boaters, with a launch site at the southern end of the lake as well as access from the Magalloway River or the Androscoggin. Thirty primitive campsites are scattered about the lake on its shoreline and islands. One campsite on an island not far from the Androscoggin looked good.

We stopped paddling and let the peace of the place sink in, content to drift and cast flies. The shoreline is a wall of green, so thick with tangled vegetation a Westerner would think they were in a jungle, especially if they glided into one of the narrow coves. The lake lived up to my expectations as a wild place, and already Ed and I were planning a return trip, one where we would cross the lake (wind permitting) to the famed Rapid River, and explore it by foot. The Rapid River (on the Maine side of Umbagog) plunges for about two miles from its outlet at the lower end of Lower Richardson Lake. Known for its salmon and native brook trout, sections of the river are carefully managed, with special fly-fishing/catch and release regulations. When I told Ed how the river occasionally gives up salmon over twenty-three inches and brook trout over four pounds, he almost hopped out of the canoe and swam over. But Umbagog is a big lake, and there was no way we could explore the Rapid and motor back in a day. And like all lakes in the north country, a crossing is not to be taken lightly—winds can kick up suddenly and canoeists are especially vulnerable.

The eagle's nest we had come to see is near where the mouth of the Androscoggin and the end of the Magalloway River meet in a confusing configuration of narrow channels and marshy setbacks known as Leonard Pond, which is not a pond at all. We located the Magalloway and paddled upstream a short distance to a good vantage point for viewing the nest. Located near the top of an enormous dead pine, two eagles stood guard over the nest, one directly on it and the other at the very tip of the pine. On such a perch they could see for miles. Silhouetted against the crystal blue sky, with white heads gleaming, they looked like royal monarchs surveying their kingdom of woods and water.

We waited with another canoe party, behind a roped-off area near the eagle's pine tree, hoping we would see the six and a half foot wingspan of an eagle in flight. But both the male and the larger female were content on their perch, no doubt scanning the water for a fish that might break the surface. Although they can grab a fish by swooping down and skimming the water with their black talons, eagles prefer to scavenge for dead fish or carrion rather than hunt. At Umbagog, with its healthy population of ospreys, the eagles can steal their food, harassing an osprey on the wing until it drops its fish, which the eagle will catch deftly in mid-air.

Their nests are large and coarse, comprised of sticks and turf with pine needles as a liner, and each year more material is added, with some nests becoming enormous affairs. Eagles mate for life and will use the same nest year after year, although this pair had previously set up housekeeping on the other side of the lake, and so one never knows which side of the lake they will be on. From one to three eggs are laid, and an incubation period of about thirty to thirty-five days follows, with the female sitting on the nest while the male brings her food. When the young hatch, both parents share in feeding them. By the tenth or eleventh week, the young will take their first flight and soon become masters of the sky.

Appreciation of the majesty of bald eagles was not always evident, especially when they were blamed for loss of livestock and game animals. These eagles were even accused of carrying off small children, and were trapped, shot and poisoned. Their decline, however had more to do with loss of habitat and the use of pesticides, particularly the widespread use of DDT in the 1950s and 1960s. Other predators at the top of their food chain, such as ospreys and peregrine falcons, also were harmed by the "miracle" pesticide. DDT leached from farmers' fields into lakes and rivers and absorbed in the tissues of tiny plants and animals, which were consumed by fish. The birds of prey who subsisted mainly on the fish received highly concentrated doses of the chemical, which inhibited their capacity to produce calcium. When the birds laid their eggs, the shells were soft, and bird populations declined in alarming proportions. After a long and acrimonious battle between conservationists and agribusiness, DDT was finally banned in 1972.

While Ed kept an eye on the eagles, I scanned the atlas, noting how the Magalloway came down into Umbagog from sections of New Hampshire so remote they didn't even have proper town names, but rather were called Grants, such as Second College Grant and Dix Grant. What an area to explore! Rivers, such as the Dead Diamond River and the Swift Diamond River, have carved paths through isolated country which few flatlanders ever see. Even this lower stretch of the Magalloway looked like a great place to see wildlife, running through forest and marsh for a couple miles between the Umbagog and Route 16. So we paddled farther up the Magalloway, watching a kingbird harass a blackbird, and a kingfisher plunge into the river for a meal. A mink prowled the shoreline, darting in and out of the brush, flushing a red-winged blackbird that escaped in the nick of time.

We expected to see a moose each time we rounded a bend, but instead saw something stranger. Three men came cruising down the river in an odd looking contraption belching puffs of gray smoke and rattling like an old boiler. It was a home-made steamboat, with the furnace and steam pipe taking up most of the boat, while the men crowded in the back.

"Does she burn wood?" I hollered.

"Yup, and just about anything else we feed her," came the reply.

"Steam-powered, right?"

"Yup, and moves pretty good too."

"What's its name?"

"It's called 'I Did It,' not to be confused with Idiot."

Maybe it's not as wild as Alaska, but there's room up here for all types. Come see.

EXPLORER'S NOTES

Recommended reading

Evolution of a Valley, The Androscoggin Story, by Page Helm Jones.
We Took to the Woods, by Louise Dickenson Rich.

Canoeing and kayaking

Northern Waters Canoe and Kayak (603-447-2177).
Wild River Adventures Guide Service and Rentals (207-824-
  2608).

Guided fishing and float trips

 Jon Howe at North Country Angler (603-356-6000).

Camping on the river

Mollidgewock Campground (603-482-3373).

Camping on Lake Umbagog

Lake Umbagog National Wildlife Refuge (603-482-7795).
The Umbagog Lake Campground (603-482-7795).
Maine Department of Conservation (207-287-3061).

Other accommodation

The Balsams (1-800-255-0800).

Launch sites on the Androscoggin River to reach Lake Umbagog

From the center of Errol, on Route 26 heading southeast, just after crossing the Androscoggin River, is a dirt road that leads north about a mile to a launch site into the river. From here it's a three-mile paddle upstream to the river. Another option, if you want to cut off some paddling time, is to put in off Route 16, just north of Errol. There is no official boat launch, so look for parking on the shoulder of the road where allowed.

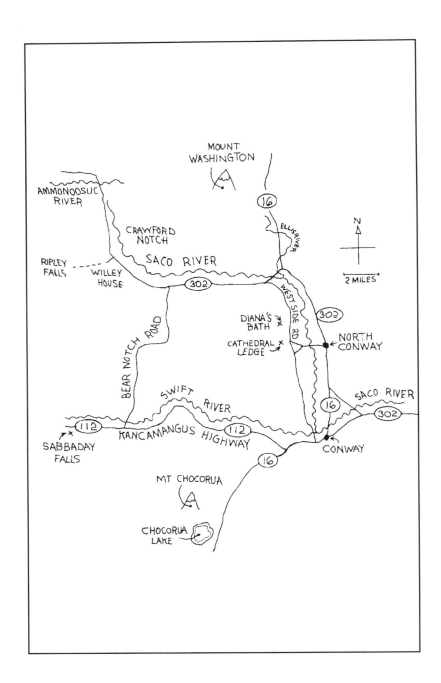

MOUNT WASHINGTON

AMMONOOSUC RIVER

CRAWFORD NOTCH

RIPLEY FALLS

WILLEY HOUSE

SACO RIVER

ELLIS RIVER

16

302

N

2 MILES

WEST SIDE RD

DIANA'S BATH

CATHEDRAL LEDGE

302

NORTH CONWAY

BEAR NOTCH ROAD

SWIFT RIVER

SACO RIVER

112

16

302

SABBADAY FALLS

KANCAMANGUS HIGHWAY

112

CONWAY

16

MT CHOCORUA

CHOCORUA LAKE

138

Brook Trout, Moose and Waterfalls—the White Mountains and Beyond

The breeze has the smell of rain in it, and I'm a half hour from my car on the wrong side of the river. Big fat drops come smacking down against the wide leaves of striped maple that grow thickly near the river bank. A minute later the sky opens up, sending a torrent down onto the river, the breeze making patterns of shifting sheets of rain. The rhythmic pounding of water and the sweeping play of the wind is not unpleasant. I peel my shirt off, stuff it in my soaking pack, and enjoy rain on bare skin. With nowhere to hide from the rain, I figure I'd enjoy it, even embrace it on this warm and humid summer day.

I'd been fishing this upper stretch of the Saco half the morning, not far from Conway, and had caught only one ten-inch brook trout, and that was on my first cast. It hit a muddler minnow on a sinking line in a wide stretch of river next to the road. When trout cooperate right off the bat, you can't help think it's going to be your lucky day, and I prepared for more action. But two hours later, and many offerings of dry flies, streamers and nymphs (two of which are still in a tree), I began to doubt my fly-fishing ability. If nothing else, angling is humbling, especially when you begin to think you've got trout figured out.

I continue to fish in the rain, working my way slowly back to the car. But I don't want to leave. I dreamed of being here last night, and I want to keep walking, fishing, thinking random thoughts. I recall a feeder stream I had seen the prior year, not too far from where I am. It came out of dark woods of hemlock and maple, whose shade made the stream cooler than the open river. Because of its small size, few anglers would have noticed it or bothered to bushwack up it. But that was the very thing that attracted me to it.

I decide to give it a try, first stopping at the car to exchange my fly rod for a spinning rod. In a narrow brook, lined with brush, an ultra-light spinning rod will allow for flick-of-the-wrist casts, and hopefully keep me out of the trees. Roll casting with a fly rod might work, but I'm no purist, and since I fish for fun rather than fashion, switching rods has become habit.

Now, almost at the mouth of the stream, the rain turns to drizzle, then stops, the earth steaming. A sudden summer rain like this one, especially one that is short-lived, can create fantastic fishing conditions. Earthworms, caterpillars and insects are washed into the river, inciting sluggish trout to cruise up from hiding places and feed. Even more important for the angler, the raindrops break the river's smooth surface and discolor its waters, assisting the angler in not being seen or heard. I'm convinced that trout are more easily spooked than we could ever imagine, feeling our footsteps and seeing our movements from great distances. They have a kind of natural radar that requires incredible stealth to penetrate, particularly in the low-water conditions of summer.

The stream is smaller than I remembered it, in fact I almost go right by it, hidden by vegetation. Pushing aside ostrich ferns and alders, I glance at its waters, tinged with a bit of brown from runoff. It varies in width from six feet to three feet. Depth is more important though, and in between the three-inch runs over riffles I can see a couple of slick pools that promise deeper waters. It is a perfect brook trout habitat, where a ten-inch trout would be a granddaddy.

Casting where the current sweeps a portion of the stream beneath the bank, a small brookie hits my spinner. It's only seven inches long, but fishing is relative, and on this stream that was a nice-sized fish. And sometimes, as it feels now, the setting is more important than the size of the fish. Being alone on a woodland brook gives one the feeling of being just another hunter in nature, like the otter, mink and heron. The intimacy of the water demands total attention, where everything is forgotten except stalking the trout. Many anglers, myself included, will trade large fish for a secluded setting, as long as the stream holds trout. There's got to be trout.

Trout have been around for about a hundred million years, and since the first man and women walked the earth, some of us have had a passion for these sleek cousins to the salmon. Maybe more than a passion. Can you love a fish? If love makes you do inexplicable things, then trout fit the bill. Some of us miss important deadlines, skip work, get in trouble with the spouse, catch pneumonia, and spend way too much money, all in an effort to bond with a fish. Catching them is secondary, but the hunt is everything. Magic can happen when an angler leaves our world and enters the trout's. Maybe that's because their world is so pure and simple. They need the cleanest, coldest and clearest water, found only in habitats so pristine it can make the heart sing.

With the stream so small I avoid walking in it, instead following it upstream, letting the vegetation screen me from any fish. Another small trout hits about a quarter mile upstream, and I see a handful of others chase my lure before dashing back to their lair. Most of the brookies seem to prefer hiding under a tangle of tree roots, so when I see a deep hole adjacent to the exposed roots of a large maple, I take extra precautions and creep the last couple yards before casting.

When my spinner hits the water I gasp. What looks like a submarine cruises out from the darkness of the roots, takes a look at the spinner, then turns and fades back under the bank. Fourteen inches? Maybe fifteen? Whatever the size, I cannot believe a fish that big can live in a stream so small.

I lift the rod to cast again but stop. No, this time I will not let my tendency toward impatience rule. I'll rest this hole, let the fish forget about what it saw, and then return. I study the pool and the root system, convinced that the trout became spooked because the lure passed too quickly from the shaded water into an open spot where pale light filters through the maples, dappling the surface. In a stream this small, escape and hiding is paramount for a fish's survival, and surely this trout is extremely wary, staying in the darkest recesses of the stream, venturing out only if food is substantial enough for the energy and risk expended.

To keep myself away from the hole, I look at my watch, telling myself I will not come back until a half hour has passed.

I fish upstream awhile, glance at my watch when I figured the allotted time has passed, and see that only ten minutes have elapsed. Rather than go farther upstream, I turn back, wanting to be within sight of the hole. The trout's not going to get up and walk away, but still I want to be close. Maybe another angler will come, I worry. Maybe I'm getting paranoid. I'm not a smoker but if I had a cigarette, I'd light it up, concentrating on every puff—anything to keep me from racing back to the hole. Instead, I look around the woods, rain water dripping off trees, wet moss glistening in the light. Above, clouds in broken patches glide by, and the sun makes an appearance one minute, rain threatening the next. I think that if it does rain, I'd get the fish for sure. But who can wait with a big trout so close? I look at my watch. Fifteen minutes have gone by. It's enough.

Moving away from the stream, I circle back through the woods, wanting to approach the hole from the downstream side, knowing the trout will be facing upstream. If trout have a blind spot, it's directly behind them. When I'm near its lair I approach slowly. I figure I'll only get one cast; either he will take a swipe at the spinner or be spooked for good. The cast will have to perfect, landing well ahead of the hole, with time for the lure to sink and then twirl by his hideout. If the cast is not directly down the alley of the stream, then I can kiss the fish goodbye. There's a two-foot-wide open lane above the stream, and on either side of that branches crowd over the water. Just below the hole a root extends half way out over the stream. Hook a branch or a root and it's real trouble. I'd have to cut my line from twenty feet back, tie on another lure and hope the next cast doesn't get tangled in the line from the first.

Chances are the trout gets spooked either way. And to make things tougher, a fallen tree lies across the stream between me and the hole, which I've got to cast over.

The fishing Spirit, luck or fate is good to me, though. The cast is true, and I literally suck in a breath when I see the shadow emerge from the tangled tree roots. I watch in what seems like slow motion. The trout looks like a shark cruising out from a submerged cave. It takes the lure and I set the hook just as it begins to curl back to the tree roots. Water explodes. I can't see the fish, nor feel it. With so many tree roots I don't play it, but instead run to it, reeling like crazy as I go, passing the pole from hand to hand as I scramble over the fallen tree.

At the hole I feel the fish throb on the end of the line, then see it sulking at the bottom. He is a monster. Only five feet separates us. It's not a matter of fighting the fish—there's no room—I just want to get him clear of the roots. I step into the hole, get my net under the water, and awkwardly try to guide the fish toward me. It bolts up to the surface and rolls. With heart pounding, I pull back on the rod, drawing him closer, then scoop upward with the net as fast as I can.

It works. I scramble to the bank drenched in sweat, glad there was no one else around to see how strange the whole thing must have looked. I measure the brook trout, almost seventeen inches. Its belly is tinged orange and on its flanks are beautiful bright red dots below a darkly marbled back. The jaw is hooked, and it really does look like a shark. For how long, I wonder, did it live in the hole among the tangle of tree roots? For how long did it ambush passing minnows, feed on smaller trout, and swallow crayfish whole? Did it come up from the river at some point, find this tree stump, and set up camp, fat and happy, never seeing any anglers?

I sit on the bank, admiring the fish, smiling. Years from now, I'll still remember everything about these few minutes, and that's what keeps the kid in us alive.

* * * *

Another favorite river of mine starts near the headwaters of the Saco up along Route 302. While the Saco flows to the southwest, the Ammonoosuc flows in the opposite direction, heading northwest into the drainage of the Connecticut River. It was while fishing the Ammonoosuc that I realized just how numerous moose have become. In fact it was a bit spooky poking through thick vegetation along the banks of the river wondering if there was a 1,200-pound moose around the bend. Like newly formed craters, moose tracks had churned up the alder thickets, and it was clear the Ammonoosuc was one of their prime feeding grounds.

The Algonkian Indian tribes called them "twig eaters," and they prefer white birch, striped maples, aspen, willow and mountain ash. They will even eat balsam fir. Although deer and moose browse may look similar, one clear distinguishing feature is that moose will browse up to seven feet above the ground, while deer will browse below four feet. Another way to determine if moose are in the area, besides locating the six-inch heart-shaped tracks, is to look for antler rubs on small trees. Again, they look like those of a deer, but the moose rub will be up near the top of a man's head, rather than below the waist. Bull moose also do something deer do not, and that is to make rub pits or wallows in the mud which they urinate in. This serves as a warning to other bulls that the territory is taken, but the cows are attracted to the pits, often rolling in the mud.

With the moose population exploding, they are seen as a nuisance to some. Just ask the man profiled recently in a local newspaper as having a bad "moose day." He hit one on the way to work, which damaged the car, then while heading home he hit another, finishing the car off. In New Hampshire alone there are over 200 collisions with moose a year, some of them fatal to the driver. Even with hunting allowed in Maine and New Hampshire, the moose population continues to increase. And New England is not alone in rising moose populations— the upper Midwest, the Rockies, and the Pacific Northwest are also seeing increases.

To get the full measure of just how big a moose is, it's best to convert measurements of feet and inches into a more visual picture. For example, a large moose's shoulders would fit inside the first floor of your home, but part of its head and antlers would protrude into the second floor. And a full-grown man could lie down comfortably between the spread of a bull moose's antlers.

With these dimensions in my head I was a little uncomfortable bushwacking my way along the river—the last thing I wanted to do was surprise a bull. But good fishing can make you brave (or foolish), and the Ammonoosuc has some fine brook-trout fishing in its upper reaches, and rainbows farther downstream. The river is clean, and easily accessible from Route 302, with enough sections that pull away from the road to give the angler a little solitude—or an encounter with a moose.

The same rivers and streams that delight us with trout and moose are perhaps most appreciated for the cascading waterfalls in the woods at the end of narrow footpaths. There are literally dozens of falls, but my three favorites are Diana's Bath (an easy walk from West Side Road in North Conway), Beecher Cascade (a easy walk from Route 302 by Crawford Depot), and Gibbs Falls (a steep but easy walk from Route 302, also near Crawford Depot). But be warned that the growth of North Conway makes it harder and harder to find wild places in the Saco River Valley, and you will have company at all of these falls.

Sometimes, however, when traveling with a family, you have to balance the urge for pushing into remote country with the limitations of small children. When I visit the region with my family, I simply accept that the places we visit are not as wild as I'd like, but a half loaf is better than none at all.

That's the way I feel about Diana's Bath, a beautiful series of small falls but one that attracts crowds. I avoid it on the weekends, but during the week I've had some great days there, watching my kids splash about in the smooth, sculptured pools. No matter how cold the water, I always go in, loving the invigorating feeling—once the shock wears off. Samuel Adams Drake in 1881 described the falls as pouring into "basins they have hollowed out. It is these curious, circular stone cavities, out of which the freshest and cleanest water constantly pours, that give the cascade the name Diana's Bath." The walk to the falls from the road is only a half mile, and the trail rises gradually, passing by impressively large hemlocks and white pines.

Another good family choice is to enjoy the view from Cathedral Ledge, located just south of Diana's Bath where River Road meets West Side Road. You can either drive to the top of the ledge or walk on a steep woods trail. Once at the summit the panorama of the Saco Valley is superb, and the fencing takes some of the worry (but not all) of bringing children to the top. Rock climbers actually ascend the vertical face of the ledge, which looks like it would be impossible to scale.

Families may also want to consider making a loop of the region, by taking West Side Road north to Route 302, then route 302 eastward to Bear Notch Road, which cuts over the mountain range separating the upper stretch of the Saco from the Swift River to the south. The road twists and turns for nine miles, offering many scenic views before it meets with the Kancamagus Highway (Route 112) at the Swift River. More family discoveries await here, such as Sabbaday Falls located a couple miles to the west on the Kancamagus. There is a parking lot by the side of the road, and a ten-minute walk will bring you to the series of falls that has carved out a small gorge.

Back on the Kancamagus (heading eastward), be sure to pull over at one of the many rest stops and explore the Swift River, or better yet float the river. There are dozens of places to do so, from the shallow riffles near the Bear Mountain Notch Road to the deeper pools of the Rocky Gorge Scenic area. At Rocky Gorge you can cross the river on a footbridge and explore Falls Pond, a picturesque pond surrounded by dense spruce and hemlocks. Or you can explore more of the Swift River—an exceptionally clear stream that makes swimming with goggles a visual treat. Just a bit downstream is the Lower Falls Recreation Area, with huge boulders and waterfalls.

The only problem with completing this loop drive is that it brings you into North Conway, with its traffic and hundreds of shops. But if you love the back roads, and want to extend your ramble, try heading south on Route 16 into Tamworth. There you will find great back roads to "get lost" on and good fishing in the Swift River (a different Swift River than the one on the Kancamagus).

Chocura Lake is a great canoeing destination, and one of the most scenic places in all New England. It's nestled in the shadow of Chocorua Mountain, and the mountain reflects off the water on calm days. (Chocorua Mountain can be climbed from trail heads such as the Piper Trail on Route 16, or from the Kancamagus Highway at Champney Falls. The hike might be too difficult for young children.) The 222-acre lake does not allow motorboats, so you can paddle in silence, and the kids will enjoy paddling beneath a small bridge and exploring adjacent Little Lake. The entire region is a good bet for introducing children to the outdoors. It gives them a taste of the wild places without the hardships.

EXPLORER'S NOTES

Notes on the White Mountains

West Side Road (on the west side of the Saco River) will allow you to bypass the congestion of Route 16 in North Conway.

All the waterfalls mentioned in the text are easy to find except Diana's Bath. It's located on West Side road about seventenths of a mile north from where River Road crosses the Saco near Echo Lake State Park and Cathedral Ledge. There are two fenced-in meadows with a dirt road running between them heading west. You can park on the shoulder of this road.

White Mountain National Forest Service can provide hiking information (603-447-5448).

Dozens and dozens of campgrounds, hotels, condos, and B&Bs are available. Call the Conway Village Chamber of Commerce (603-447-2639).

Trout streams

Blue-ribbon trout streams near North Conway include the following:

Ammonoosuc River—lots of brookies in the upper reaches, rainbows mix in farther downstream.

Saco River—runs from Route 302, south into North Conway then west into Maine. Productive fly-fishing-only section just west of the center of North Conway.

Swift River—located along the Kancamagus highway; best to hike away from the road and look for secluded areas with cover.

Ellis River—located to the north of North Conway, the Ellis River is a glacial stream with some very big rainbows in its boulder-strewn water. Portions are set aside for fly-fishing only.

North Country Anglers in North Conway can steer you in the right direction and suggest the right flies (603-356-6000).

STEP STONE FALLS

FALL RIVER

FROSTY HOLLOW RD.

165
FARRIS BROOK

WOOD RIVER

OLD NOOSENECK RD.

OLD NOOSENECK RD.

N

DAM

TO LONG POND

138

HOPE VALLEY

3

DAM

3

WYOMING POND

DAM

SWITCH ROAD

DAM

WOODVILLE RD.

WOODVILLE

ALTON POND OR WOOD RIVER POND

ALTON

DAM

91

TO ROCKVILLE AND ROUTE 138

CANONCHET RD.

N

NORTH RD.

P

LONG POND

CLIFF

HEMLOCKS

BOULDERS

RAVINE

ELL POND

Cliffs, Rivers, Owls and Ospreys—Hiking and Canoeing in Southern Rhode Island

It was the kind of day, the kind of surroundings, that nudges you into realizing that life is a gift, not a given. I was standing on a huge cliff of granite that plunges downward to meet the deep blue waters of Long Pond. Rolling hills of white pine, hemlocks, oaks and maples stretched in all directions, and two hawks spiraled lazily above in the cloudless sky. Not even the whisper of a breeze disturbed this peace, and I lay down, using my pack for a pillow. The sun warmed my face and I drifted off into one of those catnaps that are becoming all too rare.

The fact that such a wild and tranquil place is in Rhode Island, and not northern Maine, makes Long Pond and neighboring Ell Pond all the more special, which is one reason why the area has been entered in the Registry of Natural Landmarks. Here you will find a cathedral of towering hemlocks, a deep gorge, rocky overlooks, and wild rhododendrons that line the trails. It's the kind of place to make you think twice before automatically heading to northern New England for weekend exploration.

I started my hike early that October morning, entering the Long Pond and Ell Pond Natural Areas from Canonchet Road. Although the entrance from North Road provides the most direct access to the cliffs, I wanted the longer walk where you work a bit harder for the stunning view. The beginning of the trail carried me southwestward on a narrow spine of exposed granite bedrock. Stone walls laced the woods, causing me to pause and consider the efforts of those who once grubbed out an existence from such rocky soil. No wonder the younger settlers rolled the dice and moved west, where a plow could cut through and entire prairie and not hit a single rock. Here, it seemed, there were rocks everywhere; just beneath the top layer of soil, and on it as well. Even the glaciers conspired against the settlers. A huge glacial erratic boulder, measuring twenty feet across, rested on the ridge in the same spot it came to when it slid from the ice sheet over ten thousand years ago.

I could picture a farmer clearing this land two hundred years ago, the earth coughing up rocks as fast as he could plough. Large rocks were slid onto a "stone boat" and his horse would pull the sled to the site of the wall, where with the help of a neighbor or a son, each rock was fitted in place. I wondered what the farmer would think now of this second- or third-growth forest filling his field where the only trace of humans was the walls he so painstakingly built. And what would he think of the photographer I saw ahead on the trail, perched under a black sheet with an old-fashioned camera on a tripod, patiently waiting for the perfect shot of sunlight to illuminate the rock wall? And what would he think of the two hikers that came bounding down the trail heading toward Ashville Pond, skipping over the rocks with the energy of youth?

I know what I thought of the hikers and the photographer. The photographer ignored my greeting, answering my ques-

tions in monotone "yes's" and "no's," with no time for a smile.
My encounter with the hikers was altogether different. They
had just come from the cliff overlook, and inspiration was in
their voice as they described what lay ahead of me on the trail. I
noticed they had no pack, no water, and showed not the least
fatigue. Even later when I met them coming back from Ashville
Pond, they still hiked easily, with an equal measure of good
cheer for a fellow traveler in God's kingdom.

About a mile down the trail the trees abruptly turned from
mixed deciduous to almost all hemlocks, and the air was notice-
ably cooler, with a dank, earthy smell. A couple of the hemlocks
were real granddaddies, towering into the heavens. Oh, what I
would give for entire tracks of forest with mature, virgin trees,
the kind Champlain saw when he explored the new world and
recorded that they gave the woods a park-like appearance! In
William Wood's remarkable first-hand account of New England in the 1630s, he too noted that "the timber of the country
grows straight and tall, some trees being twenty, some thirty
foot high, before they spread forth their branches." With such a
thick canopy overhead, combined with the native practice of
burning the undergrowth in the fall for better hunting, Wood
wrote that "there is scarce a bush or bramble or any cumber-
some underwood to be seen in the more champion ground." In
these mature forests that Wood and Champlain traversed, trees
of two hundred, three hundred and even four hundred years of
age were not uncommon.

The old growth forests, however, didn't last long against the
settlers' hunger for cleared land. By 1900, approximately 80%
of the land was field or meadow, and almost every acre in

southern New England had been logged at least once for lumber or pasture. Naturalists at the turn of the century were warning of the fearful consequences if New England were completely deforested. Today, when we walk through woods, we see that the trees are relatively young. Only an occasional specimen, like the ones before me at Long Pond, date back more than a hundred years.

But there's optimism that the forest will work its magic, even on the part of Bob Leverett, an old-growth tree expert. He told me that even though the woods we walk are still relatively young, "there are maturing stands of trees that provide inspiration and are suggestive of the great trees of early colonial New England." He's right, and these few hemlocks on the south side of Long Pond do in fact convey the mystical feeling that only nature's grandeur can. Charles Darwin put it best when he wrote, "Among the scenes which are deeply impressed on my mind, none exceed in sublimity the primeval forests undefaced by the hand of man ... no one can stand in solitudes unmoved, and not feel that there is more in man than the mere breath of this body."

Beneath the hemlocks are scattered rhododendrons and a jumble of rocks with little nooks and crannies. I thought of timber rattlesnakes. For the rattlesnake, a rocky forested hillside with a southern exposure is essential as winter habitat. There are still a few timber rattlers holding out in pockets of New England, but I've never seen one, even though I hike weekly and have covered thousands of miles. Not so in William Wood's time:

"Now that I may be every way faithful to my readers in this work, I will as fully and truly relate to you what is evil and of most annoyance to the inhabitants ... . That which is most injurious to the person and life of man is a rattlesnake, which is generally a yard and half long, as thick in the middle as the small of a man's leg. Her poison lieth in her teeth, for she hath no sting. When any man is bitten by any of these creatures, the poison spreads so suddenly through the veins and so runs to the heart that in one hour it causeth death unless he hath the antidote to expel the poison, which is a root called snakeweed. It is their desire in hot weather to lie in the paths where the sun may shine on them, where they will sleep so soundly that I have known four men stride over one of them and never awake her."

Today the timber rattlesnake—as well as the copperhead—have been reduced to such few numbers that both are endangered species, and it is illegal to kill, harass or possess one. All snakes should be left alone, and it is sometimes difficult to distinguish between the poisonous and the non-poisonous. But if you are close enough to see that the head is triangular, stay clear—that's a distinguishing feature of rattlers and copperheads.

Separating Long Pond from Ell Pond is a wet area at the base of a gorge. I crossed the trickle of a stream on a double-log footbridge, then climbed through the far end of the ravine on strategically placed rocks that form a crude stairway through sheer rock walls. Once at the top of the gorge I came to a T-intersection, and first went to see the partial view of Ell Pond (an L-shaped bog) and then picked my way through boulders and enormous rhododendrons on the trail that leads to North

Road. I saved the best for the last, finally making my way to the dramatic rock outcrop above Long Pond, where I took my nap.

Upon waking, I recall staring into the blue sky overhead, wondering if future generations would be able to do the same. It's impossible not to think of the destruction of the ozone layer when you gaze into the heavens on a clear day. In 1996 the ozone hole over Antarctica widened to a size roughly equal to the combined area of the United States and Canada, at 7.7 million square miles. We know that man-made chemicals used in aerosols and refrigeration are responsible for its depletion, but getting them banned is another thing. Under the 1987 Montreal Protocol, the world's governments agreed to phase out these chemicals, but the measures don't take full effect until the second half of the twenty-first century.

And so I lay there, closing my eyes in a silent prayer that people put the health of the planet, the purity of the sky, and the restoration of our water ahead of creature comforts, consumerism, and short-term personal gain. You might think my thoughts would be filled with gloom, but over the last couple of years I've detected a change in people, an enlightened change, espousing the idea that the earth is worth sacrificing for, that the earth is more important than the individual, and that protecting this earth is as natural as protecting our children. And I detect a consciousness that what we call nature is part of a whole which includes humankind, and that all things are interrelated.

Lying quietly on hilltops or mountaintops can make you think such thoughts. High places can stir the spirit, and we must go to them more often to reflect, and possibly leave re-

newed and invigorated. Whether its Kineo or Katahdin, or
some lesser hill like the bluff at Long Pond, a few quiet moments alone up high will connect you with the more important,
elemental things that we miss in daily life.

Another place which has this effect on me is on the water or
near the water, and I left the hilltop to spend the remaining
hours of the day by the Wood River.

* * * *

The Wood River gathers its strength from the many feeder
streams that join its song just north of Route 165 in the Arcadia
Management Area. The stretch between Stepstone Falls and
Route 165 is perhaps its most scenic run, with the Ben Utter
Trail paralleling most of this section. Here the river is still but a
stream, dashing over rocks, in a narrow course that tumbles
through sun-dappled forest.

I followed the trail northward, finding the murmur of
moving water by my side better than the best music. The sunlight filtering through the treetops caused small patches of
water to glisten white in the afternoon sun, a perfect contrast to
the shiny green leaves of mountain laurel that lined the trail.
The river drops in a series of one-foot falls, and I watched an
elderly fly fisherman drift a nymph over a fall, then down to the
base of a pool. The line straightened, he set the hook with a
little flick of the wrist, and a small brook trout rolled on the
river's surface. He played the fish for a moment, then with the
aid of a net held the trout steady, removed the hook and
released his catch.

It was a pleasure to watch him fish. He moved as slowly as a
great blue heron, stalking its prey, scanning every pool, every

eddy. In fact he was so absorbed in his pursuit he passed by without noticing me resting beneath a pine. When a hobby calls for all your attention, as trout fishing on a stream does, you can lose yourself in the activity, forgetting your surroundings, the time, and your problems—only the river and you. It's a sure way for a man or woman to feel the boy or girl locked away inside.

What a joy to be out wading in a river, peering around logs, deciding on placement of your cast! I thought of all the fishing I'd done with my friend Cogs. How we'd decide who would take the upstream section, who would go down, and what time we would later meet. But time means little on a river, and I can't remember when we ever met at the appointed hour. If the trout were biting we simply had to stay out longer. If the trout were not feeding we did the same, reasoning that just one more pool, just one more bend in the river would yield a strike. And when we did meet, ah, that was almost as good as the fishing, to hear what happened to your partner. Spills and mishaps in the river, the one that got away, or the sighting of a mink or night heron, these were the stories we looked forward to after a spending a few hours alone.

I resumed my walk and came upon an old mill site, with mill race, granite blocks and little waterfall. No matter how small the stream, in New England it was most likely dammed for a mill. I pictured a grist mill or lumber mill operating here, horse and buggy pulling up to unload supplies. What stories lie beneath the humus and fallen leaves, what dreams and hopes of the man who ran this little mill? Did he work around the clock, or did he close up early on the first warm day in May to go fishing?

As beautiful as the man-made falls by the old mill site are, the natural ones at Stepstone Falls, about a mile upstream, are even better. The river glides over water-worn rock ledges in a series of gentle steps beneath crimson swamp maples. Is there anything as visually pleasing as a pure river splashing in the sun?

* * * *

In the towns south of the Ben Utter Trail, the Wood River deepens a bit and is known as Rhode Island's premier canoeing river, with a combination of quick-water and flat-water paddling through quiet countryside. Beaver, otter, wood duck and heron live along the river, and just about every fish found in southern New England swims in its waters. Oxbows, marshes, tiny islands and hidden ponds await discovery for Wood River paddlers. It is not a particularly big river, and because of its narrow course there are blow-downs which sometimes block a canoeist's passage. There are also many dams, so that knowledge of the river is essential for first-time paddlers.

For my education, I approached the man whose name kept coming up whenever I asked about floating the Wood River. Manny Point lives on the banks of the river, watching it flow, gauging its moods, and delighting in the wildlife that passes by his back door. For more than twenty-five years he's been guiding canoeists on the river and donating his time to conserving its health and beauty.

Manny is a short man, with a bushy beard and a small gray ponytail, who looks to be in his fifties rather than his true age, sixty-eight. When I first arrived at his home on a September morning he seemed a bit reserved, giving me the tour of his riverside acre in Wyoming, then mapping out our paddle.

"For a short ride, you can't beat the run from Barberville down here to where I live on Wyoming Pond," he said pointing to my topographical map. "It's only a couple of miles, but it's a nice stretch of water going through the woods. There's a little quick water just to make it interesting. Later you can do the stretch by Woodville, which is wider and slower."

At Barberville, we unloaded the canoe by a small dam, and he told me a story that would sober any paddler.

"Awhile back some fellas launched here during the high water of spring. They put in right below the dam and instead of shooting downstream, the hydraulics forced them under the falls. Two men died."

"Did they have lifejackets on?"

"Yup. But the water kept them in the falls. And it doesn't take long for hypothermia to weaken you in the spring."

I looked at the water below the dam. The river was almost as high as springtime conditions from recent rains, but still the current didn't look too bad—which is exactly what the victims must have thought. Looks are deceiving, especially on a river, and all it takes is a back eddy from a waterfall to suck you and your canoe into danger.

A sign had been erected at the falls instructing paddlers to launch on the other side of the street, which is where we put in. Manny said the quick water was only in a few spots, and he didn't anticipate trouble. Still he took the time to give me his three golden rules of running white water:

"Keep your paddle in the water no matter what happens, and whatever you do don't grab onto the gunnels. And remember to keep your head centered—it weighs a full eighteen pounds and if it's leaning over the side your body will follow."

I knelt in the bow and he shoved us off. We ran the little stretch of white water, making a sharp right turn through a channel, then reconnecting with the main flow. The river was so narrow that trees from either side joined together to form a low, tunnel-like canopy of foliage. Where the sun did filter through, it sparkled on singing rapids and glistening black boulders that broke the current. Even as we sped through the rapids, I noticed pocket water where trout would hold, and made a mental note to return.

The river then changed speed, with the only other tricky part at a broken dam about a three-eighths of a mile downstream. Manny directed the canoe through the Vs between submerged boulders, and before I knew it the fun was over and the river quieted down for good.

Now that we had been on the water together for a few minutes, Manny warmed up to my questions, as if the river had formed a bond between us. He told me how he founded the Rhode Island Canoe Association and how he became a registered Maine guide, leading trips down Maine's Allagash River. I asked him if the wilder Allagash made the Wood River seem second rate.

"Not at all," Manny said, "It may not be as wild, but I'm always seeing something new here. Two days ago I saw my first bald eagle on the river; it dove like a missile to get a trout. And then there's the regulars like the mink that prowls the shore near my house, and an enormous snapping turtle that must be a hundred years old that comes out every spring to lay its eggs."

I asked him how he came to be a riverman.

"I grew up in Providence but my father worked for a construction company that took him to Maine's north country. My mother would take me up to see him on weekends and we always canoed a new river. Later I became a Navy frogman, and that really got me interested in all manner of aquatics. Since then I've canoed hundreds of rivers all over America."

He paused, then cracking a smile, added, "I figured you'd be ok in the white water when I saw your canoe didn't have any big holes in it."

True praise from a riverman.

As we talked, the river slowed its flow and widened, making its way to Wyoming Pond. Painted turtles basked in the sun, and on one log I counted over twenty-five turtles packed together. A great blue heron stood motionless nearby, reluctant to give up its hunting spot.

"What's the river like upstream of where we put in at Barberville?" I asked.

"Narrow, with plenty of switchbacks, not the kind of place you should canoe alone. Try the run from Woodville Road to Alton for a great ride; that's my second favorite spot on the river."

After I dropped Manny off at his home, I took his advice and drove down to the dam at Woodville Road. A grist mill operated here in the eighteenth century, and in the late nineteenth century two mills were operating. Signs of the past grace this peaceful spot, with a couple of old mill homes still standing, and ruins of an old mill and sluiceway still evident near the waterfall. On a tree was nailed a sign stating that the river is stocked with Atlantic salmon, identified most easily by the forked tail. If you catch one under fifteen inches, be sure to release it!

I launched the canoe and settled into a rhythmic pace of slow paddling, watching the tea-colored water swirl with each dip of the paddle. One of the reasons I love canoeing is for its silence, allowing you to slip through the woods and marsh like you belong, rather than as a loud intruder. It's very different from the noisy world we live in, and infinitely more peaceful.

I'm told the stands of mountain laurel that line the banks of the river are spectacular in June, and later in the summer the iris, pickerel weed and white waterlilies add color to the greenery. But on my autumn trip it was the swamp maples that took center stage, with their brilliant shades of red, yellow and orange. Oaks, black gum, white pine and blueberry are scattered in the woods just beyond the swamp maples.

Not far from the put-in, there is a sharp channel to the left and one straight ahead. It seems like the river should go straight ahead, but don't be fooled, as I was. I found myself paddling into an ever narrowing channel that finally ended at a trickle of water passing a farm. This was once a mill race, where the water was diverted from the river to power a mill. Turn back and continue down the true channel of the river.

The river runs slowly and surprisingly deep in spots, with the occasional boulder showing to keep you on your toes. Turtles plopped off logs, and a red-tailed hawk screeched high overhead. On the left bank I passed a sandy beach with a rope swing, and gave it serious thought until I tested the water temperature with my hand. Soon the river began to spread itself into marsh, indicating I was at the upper reaches of Alton Pond (also known as Wood River Pond). Tussocks of grass grew along back coves, and standing deadwood rose like sentinels guarding the western wetlands.

This was an area of utter peace and beauty, with wood ducks winging through the marsh, as well as green heron, great blue heron, mallards, and many other birds. High above me a half dozen turkey vultures circled lazily in the blue sky. The current all but stops, and you should do the same. I took my shirt off and stretched back against the stern to enjoy the last warm days of sunshine. Something wonderful happens when you're in sync with the river, a feeling that you're meant to be here at this particular time, floating like a piece of driftwood.

When I resumed paddling it wasn't long before I reached the pond itself, complete with a strong head wind, making me glad I had rested before putting muscle into my strokes. The pond, like so many bodies of water, is a mill pond formed in the 1800s. It's a popular fishing spot, with warm-water species such as largemouth bass, pickerel and yellow perch. But on this day there was not another boat to be seen. I crossed the pond, pulling the paddle hard against the wind, then stayed close to the right shoreline before pulling out above the dam.

From where I pulled out it was just a short drive to the Great Swamp, but the sun was setting, so I left and didn't make it back until spring. But things have a funny way of working out, because it's springtime, not fall, when the Great Swamp ospreys are nesting, and they treated me to a memorable sight.

* * * *

It's hard to imagine that the Great Swamp Wildlife Management Area was once the scene of a terrible massacre. In 1675, English soldiers made a surprise attack on a Narraganset winter camp located deep within the swamp. Little did it matter that the Narragansetts were neutral during King Philip's War, which raged to the north in Massachusetts and Plymouth Colonies. The English were intent on striking a blow against the Narragansetts, fearful that they might soon join Metacom, called King Philip by the English. And so on a frigid and snowy December morning, soldiers led by a native traitor followed a narrow path into the heart of the swamp and attacked the camp, killing more than 500 Narragansetts, mostly women and children.

Now, on an early spring morning, the 3,000-acre swamp is a wondrous place of life, with the scent of newly thawed earth hanging low in the tangled woods. For many, March is known as a dark and dreary month, but here in the wetlands life is exploding. Flocks of redwing blackbirds make the morning sing, and an occasional turtle suns itself after a winter in the muck.

They say the sense of smell has the power to evoke memories, but on this morning the mewing of a catbird brings me back to the patch of woods behind my boyhood home. My brother Mark and I spent day after day there, learning through unsupervised play, absolutely free to follow our curiosity. The native Americans lived much the same way, and the Puritan English would complain of their freedom and idleness. But in my opinion the natives had it right; creative, open-minded thinking comes about when children are free to imagine, rather than being herded into structured activities. And a swamp such as this might be the best "classroom" of all.

Natives, childhood, freedom—these are the thoughts that go through my mind as I walk the entrance trail, passing holly trees that sparkle in the sun. By arriving at dawn, I have the place to myself, and plan to make a four-mile walk around the open marsh created when a dike was constructed in the 1950s. Later, I'll canoe Worden Pond, a shallow, thousand-acre pond that abuts the swamp.

Crossing an open field, I saw a kestrel with a touch of blue on its wings perched on a branch, surveying the ground for any sign of movement. The little bird, no bigger than a blue jay, didn't look like much of a predator, but I knew from experience they sometimes eat more than insects. I once saw one swoop down on a starling and kill it in a spray of feathers. But today, the kestrel I was watching seemed content to soak up the sun, and I pushed onward into the swamp.

On most trips to woods I'd consider seeing a kestrel a successful "wildlife watching" excursion. But once in a blue moon—perhaps one out of every twenty-five walks—I get lucky and am treated to a wide diversity of wildlife. This was one of those days.

Where the trail runs along the top of the dike, I watch two osprey circling high above the power lines in the middle of the marsh. They were reconstructing one of the huge nests at the top of the power-line poles. A rickety old boardwalk lay beneath the poles and I decided to walk out to shoot some pictures.

The ospreys were bringing sticks to the nest, working them into place, then flying off in search of more. They were magnificent, graceful birds, with wingspans of over four feet. It was truly a wonderful sight, especially since the birds had been all but wiped out of New England from the effects of DDT. I lay back on the boardwalk to admire their beauty and watch the show.

Suddenly one of the osprey, which was soaring directly overhead, let out a screech and flew towards a different nest that I thought was empty. It swooped low, pulling its wings in, and I heard something hiss. With the aid of binoculars I looked up to see a large brown head poking out from the mass of woven sticks. I blinked and refocused—it was a great horned owl. Apparently the owl had commandeered the osprey nest to lay its own eggs.

The osprey buzzed the nest two more times until the owl had had enough and flew off, landing on a dead tree out in the middle of the marsh. Now that it was in the open, more of its enemies joined the fray. First a small flock of crows came, mobbing the owl like a wrestling tag team until the owl gave up its roost and glided ghost-like into the forest.

I could hear the crows cawing furiously from the dark woods and wondered if the owl had turned on them. The crows had good reason to harass the bird, because in the black of night an owl will occasionally pluck a young crow from its treetop nest. The owl is one of nature's most deadly hunters, able to see at night and approach its prey silently due to the soft feathers at the front of its wings which muffle any sound. No wonder the natives considered seeing the owl a bad omen.

The crows' cawing trailed off and I was about to leave when the owl emerged from the woods and again took up its position on the dead tree. Immediately two red-tailed hawks came racing in from the north, screeching and pestering the owl in the same fashion as the crows had. I sat transfixed, watching the drama unfold as if in a movie theater when the action on the screen keeps coming.

When I left the boardwalk a half hour later the owl was back in the abandoned osprey nest, its attackers having given up and flown away. All was quiet.

The sun was warm now. I could almost feel the new season emerging, almost hear the growth of a multitude of plants, almost smell the scent of procreation. The primordial ooze had thawed and there were signs of new life everywhere. I imagined it as the first day of creation when all living things coexisted.

But the peace was just a façade. Birds and other wild creatures, like men, would battle over territory, and life and death would be random and unfair—just as it had been 300 years ago at the Great Swamp Massacre.

EXPLORER'S NOTES

Recommended reading

The Great Swamp Massacre is well-documented in *The Red King's Rebellion,* by Russell Bourne, and featured in the novel *Until I Have No Country,* by Michael Tougias. A fascinating eyewitness account can be found in *Diary of King Philip's War,* by Benjamin Church.

Canoeing on Wood River

Manny Point and his son Gary lead guided trips and shuttle service on the Wood River. Call Four-Point Canoe Outfitters (401-539-7248).

The Great Swamp

The Great Swamp Wildlife Management Area (not shown on our map) is located in South Kingston. From Route 138 turn onto Liberty Lane and follow it until it ends at railroad tracks about a mile down. Then go left on a dirt road until the end and park in by a gate (401-789-0281).

South County Tourism Council (800-548-4662).

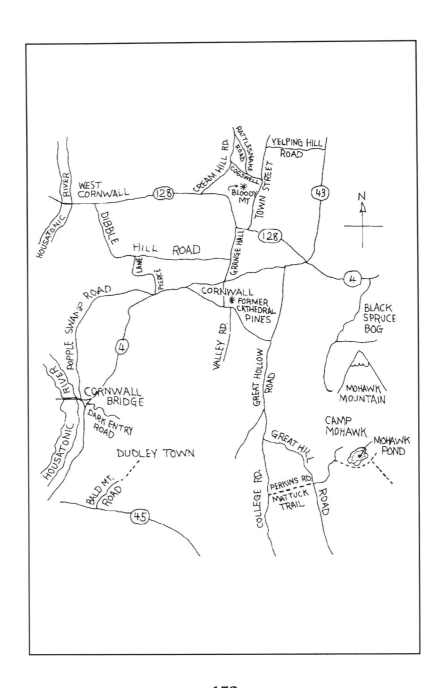

Exploring Cornwall—
Tornadoes, Mysteries
and Hidden Back Roads

My guidebook was a little out of date. It said that just outside the center of Cornwall was an enchanted area known as Cathedral Pines. The author said the white pines are so large they affect the hiker in a hushed, humbling way, and that "naturalists talk about this stand in the same awed tones that historians use to describe great Gothic cathedrals in Europe." But what I saw was devastation.

On Monday, July 10, 1989, a storm which spawned tornadoes swept down out of the northwest and cut a path diagonally across Connecticut from Canaan all the way to New Haven. Cornwall was in the path, and Cathedral Pines took a direct hit. What took 300 years to grow was gone in minutes.

An eyewitness to the storm described how the hot, muggy afternoon gave birth to the tornado: "All of a sudden the world became a strange green light and funny calm." Then the skies opened up with torrential rains, terrible wind and lightning. This happened at 4:20 pm, and by 4:30 the worst was over. Miraculously there was only one minor injury in town, but homes were damaged or destroyed and all the big trees in the village were gone.

And now, seven years later, the path of the tornado is still visible. Mountains look like they were shaved by a mad barber, the stumps of trees like stubble on a beard. The hill where Cathedral Pines stood is still a sickening sight; a few enormous pine trunks stand with tops gone, others stacked like toothpicks, all of it looking like a war zone.

How strange, I thought. Of all the places for the tornado to touch down it ripped smack through the center of the stand of oldest trees in the state, while nearby mountains of second- and third-growth trees were unscathed. Cornwall, I would learn, has its share of oddities.

* * * *

It was March, maybe not the best time for tramping in the woods, but I was desperate for forest, sick of civilization. Too many weekends in suburban Boston had left me with a good case of cabin fever—grouchy and anxious. It's simply not healthy to stay at home too long. The routine of going from home to office by car or train, often leaving in the dark and returning in the dark, can dull the senses, or worse. I needed to break the rut, get away from the familiar, away from material things, and away from things electronic—phones, computers, TV.

"Civilization," said Mark Twain, "is a limitless multiplication of unnecessary necessaries."

Before leaving home I studied a topographical map, captivated by brown contour lines, green shaded forests, and a dozen oddly named back roads and ridges that snaked through the mountains: Yelping Hill Road, The Crooked Estes, Dark Entry, Bloody Mountain and Rattlesnake Road. Again a

Cornwall oddity that one little town should have so many forboding names. But I love a good name, love to learn its origin, and love to pay the place a visit, hoping it lives up to its name. In suburbia many of the original roads and village names have been lost over time, or worse, they are replaced by more pleasing names that have no connection with the land. Mud Pond becomes Lake Crystal. Carter's Swamp is filled in, developed and re-named Maplewood Estates, where most of the maples have been cut to make room for chemically treated lawns. And then there are the builders who name their developments after the very animals they drove out or bulldozed under: Fox Hollow, Partridge Run, Buck Hill, and similar nonsense.

But in Cornwall, the names have not been changed, and when I arrived in town I researched a few in the library. Shin-bone Alley is a narrow, steep passage that scraped the underside of carriages and presumably many a shin. Yelping Hill Road was named for the sounds of the nearby fox population. (For those who have never heard the wail of a fox at night, believe me when I say it is one of the most unearthly calls you've ever heard.) Switchbacks through the narrow valley of two ridges account for Crooked Estes, but I never did learn the origin of the name Baldwin Cave.

Rattlesnake Road was named for the day in the 1740s when fifty rattlers were killed on this lane. In *Cornwall in 1801*, by Elijah Allen, I read that "the mountains and rocks afforded a safe retreat in winter season to an almost, if not quite, afford-able number of rattlesnakes. In the spring they issued out of their dens in the cavities and the rocks and spread abroad on the face of the earth. Town meeting voted to give six pence for every rattlesnake tail that should be killed. I have heard that a Mrs. Griffis went to the den of these poisonous reptiles with unshaken and firm display of heroism and fortitude uncommon to the tender and amicable difference which so highly recommended the fair sex ... and at the mouth of the den and near thereto attacked and killed large numbers of rattlesnakes. The foregoing measures, and the woods being often burnt in the spring in former years, and those eaten by hogs (which it is said) devour with avidity, all concur to make almost utter end of these poisonous reptiles at this day." (The snakes have never recovered from such practices, and today only a handful exist throughout New England.)

Mohawk Mountain is named for the Mohawk tribe, who lived to the west, in what is now New York State. They were the easternmost tribe of the Iroquois Confederacy. The Algonquian tribes of New England were enemies of the Mohawks, calling them flesh-eaters, and lived in fear of their frequent raids. In *New England's Prospect*, written by colonial settler William Wood in 1634, the Mohawks are described as fierce and fearless, and of great strength. In fact Wood credits the Algonquian hatred of the Mohawks as one reason the natives of Massachusetts originally accepted the Pilgrims and Puritans, in hopes that the English would fight against their enemies.

* * * *

It was at the base of Mohawk Mountain that I strapped on my snowshoes to see what I could do about my cabin fever. Thousands of acres of forest have been preserved at this state park, which includes Black Spruce Bog with its larch trees, leatherleaf, sheep laurel and sphagnum moss. The pitcher plant and the sundew, both carnivorous plants that trap and digest insects, grow within the acid bog soil. Mohawk Mountain itself is worth the climb (cars can also be driven to the top) where the views from the stone tower at the 1,683-foot summit stretch west into New York and north into Massachusetts. But with almost two feet of snow on the ground, I wasn't about to tackle the mountain, and instead set my sights on an outing near Mohawk Pond. (My rule of thumb for when to use snowshoes is that they assist when there is more than eight inches of snow, but slow you down in anything less.)

The wooden snowshoes with the gut webbing had hung in my closet for quite some time and soon after strapping them on I realized just how out of shape I was. First the parka came off, then the sweater, as the exertion had me huffing, puffing and heating up. But the woods were beautiful, stark, and silent, luring me deeper.

Pine, hemlock, maple, beech and oak provided dark contrast with the white snow. Some of the trees were large, but like almost every acre in New England there were no virgin trees or old growth trees like the ones that once stood at Cathedral Pines. Early settlers cleared the valleys and rolling hills for pasture and farming, and loggers did the same to the mountains. If you live in New England, go down to your town library and examine the old photographs of your town in the late 1800s. Chances are you will see an endless expanse of pasture land. The only trees to escape the axe were usually those shading roadways or in steep ravines, too difficult to log.

As I plodded onward I tried to imagine what this forest would look like if it had never been altered by man. The natives often burned the woods to improve hunting, but their fires consumed brush and low-lying vegetation rather than the big trees. Early explorers such as Champlain and Captain John Smith recorded that the forests of New England were park-like and open enough to march an army through. Towering chestnut, ash, oak, walnut, and maple formed a canopy overhead, blocking out the sun.

A couple of hours of snowshoeing had me ravenous, and I parked myself under a hemlock tree, spreading a plastic garbage bag from my pack over a log to sit on. I drank mightily from my water jug, and a PBJ never tasted so good. I thought that maybe by sitting quietly I might see a fox, deer or porcupine, but nothing disturbed the stillness. Once, while at Quabbin resting by the reservoir, I was lucky enough to see three coyotes trot along the shoreline in late afternoon. Since I was seated and presumably upwind they passed close by, never even looking my way. The size of the coyotes surprised me: I estimated their average weight at forty pounds, about twice as large as a fox. It's thought the coyote first moved into New England from the west in the 1920s. The eastern coyote is larger than its western cousins, perhaps because they might have interbred with wolves in southern Canada.

But no animals showed themselves to me on this day, nor for that matter did any birds, except for two crows who cawed loudly from the top of a nearby pine. Crows are known for their intelligence, and I wondered if they were hanging around, waiting for me to leave so they could swoop down to my lunch spot in search of crumbs. I'd read how members of a crow family were observed collectively tormenting otters, sometimes pulling their tails to distract them so that one of the crows could steal fish parts. Crows work well together in teams, but why they roost in such large numbers, often returning to the same spot year after year, is something of mystery. Certainly there is truth in such conventional theories as sharing body warmth, being better able to warn each other of predators, and following smarter crows to the best foraging areas. But this could be accomplished in much smaller groups. Perhaps crows gather for the same reason people do, simply to be together.

The rest of my snowshoeing was uneventful but proved to be the right prescription for cabin fever. Back at the car I was exhausted, but it was a physical kind of weariness rather than mental, and I'll take that trade-off any day.

* * * *

Dudleytown. Some said to stay away, it's a cursed ghost town, where bad things have happened and continue to happen. Others merely laughed, saying the curse is an exaggeration of events from days gone by. Either way the Dudleytown section of Cornwall intrigued me, and not just its mystery. It is also a wild area, where the forest has swallowed up this mountain village, and today it's a nature sanctuary.

First the strange history. Settlement of Dudleytown began in 1738, when farmers began working the land and later engaged in the practice of burning wood for charcoal to supply the nearby smelting furnaces. Scratching out a living was difficult, and life was hard. The fact that Dudleytown is located on a high plateau in the shadow of mountains certainly didn't help the farming, and part of the curse can simply be written off to its poor geological location. But those who believe in the curse say the series of deaths and "derangements" make it more than just an abandoned hill town.

Calamity befell Dudleytown citizens even after they left the village. For example, the Carter family left Dudleytown and set up a homestead near Binghamton, New York, where natives massacred part of the family and carried others off into captivity. Meanwhile, back at Dudleytown an unknown epidemic was said to have killed a number of villagers in 1813. The population continued to dwindle as residents left for employment in nearby cities and farmers headed west. The handful of villagers who remained saw the handwriting on the wall, as abandoned homes fell into disrepair and no new families moved in.

The last family living in Dudleytown was the Brophys, husband, wife and two sons. In *Legendary Connecticut,* author David Philips chronicles their misfortune:

"The boys were discovered stealing some sleigh robes down in Cornwall and rapidly left the area, just ahead of the law. Their mother worked too hard, ate too little and died of tuberculosis soon after her sons' flight. Finally, in 1901, after his house burned to the foundation, Brophy threw in the towel: he left Dudleytown forever."

That might have been the end of the village's bad luck had not Dr. William C. Clark, a prominent physician and professor at a New York City medical school, taken a liking to the secluded hills of Dudleytown. Philips describes how Clark came to Dudleytown over a series of summers and built his cottage with his own hands. When the cottage was complete, his wife joined him and they spent many happy summers before misfortune or the curse struck. One summer Dr. Clark had to return to New York for a few days, leaving his wife alone at the Dudleytown cottage. Philips writes that Dr. Clark returned to Cornwall within thirty-six hours.

"But when nobody met him at the station, he hurriedly walked to the opening at Dark Entry Road and plunged into the shadowy woods. Except for the hooting of owls, all was quiet as he entered the clearing where his summer cottage stood. No sign of life greeted him as he ran, terrified, across the lawn to the cabin. But as he pushed open the front door, which had been left slightly ajar, he heard a sound that he would never forget. From an upstairs room came the maniacal, uncontrolled laughter of one who had taken leave of her senses. During his absence, his wife had gone quite mad."

(*A History of Cornwall Connecticut,* written in 1926, tells of an even worse ending to this story, saying that Mrs. Clark's "mind began to wabble, and she took her own life.")

Maybe the Clarks should have listened to the local whisperings about the "cursed place." Maybe they should have been tipped off to trouble by the name Dark Entry Road. And maybe I should reconsider my tramp in the woods there.

Cornwall residents I spoke with are split on their feelings about Dudleytown. Some agree with historian Paul H. Chamberlain Jr., who wrote that the curse is really a myth, and that Dudleytown's dark, isolated location in the shadow of mountains had more to do with its demise than any misfortunes. But others are not so sure. One old timer said, "Don't go up there. Only a few strangers poke around in those hills; none of us who live here have anything to do with the place." Another told me of her last outing to Dudleytown, describing how she and a friend went for a walk during a January thaw, with bright blue skies and extraordinary mild temperatures.

"But as soon as we reached the old cellar holes, the sky suddenly darkened, the temperature plunged, and it snowed so furiously we could not see. We took shelter in a cellar hole, but when the storm didn't blow over we figured we better get out of there. It was a whiteout; we couldn't see the trail, but kind of felt our way along. A half mile from the cellar holes, back near the entrance, the wind died down, the sun came out, and the temperature moderated. Haven't been back since, and don't suppose I will."

I was more curious about the place than ever and took a look at my topographical map one more time. The site of Dudleytown lies just to the east of the Housatonic River and is bordered by Route 4 to the north and Route 45 to the south. Woodbury Mountain looms over it from the east, Bald Mountain and Dudleytown Hill lock it in on the south, and the Coltsfoot Range parallels its northwestern border. I was surprised to see that up until recently the Appalachian Trail cut through Dudleytown on its way to Mohawk State Forest. Surely the trail wasn't re-routed because of the curse, but one never knows.

Rather than gain access to Dudleytown via Dark Entry Road, I choose Bald Mountain Road as a less forbidding place to begin my hike. While strapping on my snowshoes I noticed there were no other tracks in the snow. I began to wonder if maybe it would be better to take this tramp with a friend rather than alone.

But once inside the woods, all thoughts of gloom and doom were replaced by an appreciation for its silence and simple beauty. A white birch stood in beautiful contrast with the dark green hemlocks, and stone walls from the hands of the first Dudleytown settlers graced the forest. Farther down the path two large white birches leaned against one another directly over the trail, forming a handsome archway to travel through. A few cellar holes were visible and a clear mountain stream bubbled down a hillside.

While so much of Cornwall's forest had been leveled or at least damaged by the tornado, I found Dudleytown's woods to be unscathed. In fact, the farther I snowshoed the more I liked these woods.

Still, I paid close attention to the paths I was on, making a hand-drawn map so I could easily retrace my steps later in the day. The warnings and the legend of the curse were in the back of my mind. Hiking here in the day is one thing, being lost at night would be quite another.

EXPLORER'S NOTES

Recommended reading

Ghost Towns of New England, by Fessenden Blanchard, and *Legendary Connecticut,* by David Philips, both provide entertaining anecdotes and legends of Dudleytown.

Lodging and camping in Cornwall

College Hill Farm is an authentic 1808 central-chimney colonial farmhouse situated on twenty acres adjoining Mohawk State Forest. Three guest chambers are furnished with family antiques, and the "keeping room" has a walk-in fireplace and beehive bake oven. Baths are shared and the owner has pets (860-672-6762).

Cornwall Inn & Restaurant in Cornwall Bridge has twelve rooms and a pool (800-786-6884).

Hilltop Haven, with private baths, is on sixty-three acres in West Cornwall (860-672-6871).

Litchfield Hills Travel Council (860-567-4506).

Situated on the banks of the river is the state-run Housatonic Meadows Campground (860-672-6772).

Selected trails and back roads

Mohawk State Forest has numerous trails on Mohawk Mountain, near Mohawk Pond, and along the Mattatuck Trail. The Mattatuck Trail is thirty-five miles long, part of which passes along an old road, Perkins Road, now closed to motor vehicles. Almost all the back roads in Cornwall are scenic, and provide opportunities for wildlife viewing. Consider bicycling these back roads in the spring and fall.

Canoeing

Clarke Outdoors is located on Route 7 in West Cornwall, offering canoe and kayak rentals, white-water rafting in the spring, and instructions for beginners all the way to white-water experts (860-672-6365).

(A more extensive summary of the region is found at the end of the chapter on the Housatonic River.)

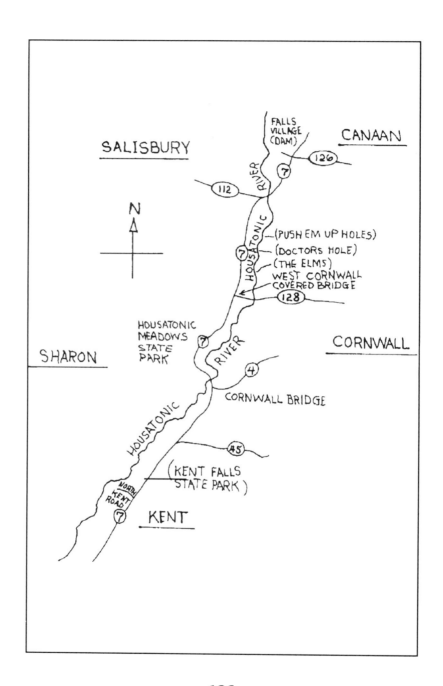

The Housatonic River

The Housatonic River, which in the Mahican language means "The Place Beyond the Mountains," rises from three ponds near Pittsfield, Massachusetts, and flows southward 150 miles, through Connecticut, all the way to Long Island Sound. Passing through flood plains and steep forested hills, it's a river of many moods. Unfortunately for my companion Giles and I, the mood of the river on our day of canoeing could only be described as surly. Two days of drenching rain had the river running high, swift and muddy. Although it was the middle of June, the river looked like it does after the spring snow melt.

With the aid of Clarke Outdoors, from whom we rented our canoes, we mapped out a run of about eighteen miles, starting below the power station at Falls Village and ending at the town of Kent. The two guidebooks we were using gave plenty of warning about the river's power during high water. Ken Weber, in his excellent book, *Canoeing Massachusetts, Rhode Island and Connecticut,* writes that "the section between Falls Village and Cornwall, which includes a picturesque covered bridge at West Cornwall, is a favorite of whitewater canoeists. That segment is not included here because it requires skills beyond those of the average paddler and also because it cannot be run at all during low-water months." *The AMC River Guide* describes the stretch as smooth water alternating with

Class I and II rapids until the covered bridge at West Cornwall is reached seven and a half miles downstream. It warns of the bridge as follows:

"CAUTION! There is a long wooden bridge here, and one should pull out well above it to look over the 1/4 mile of rapids (Class II–III) which starts just above the bridge and runs down to the corner below. This can be dangerous (Class IV) at high water."

The guide also notes a tricky corner just below the rest area from the powerhouse at Falls Village. Giles and I, just fifty feet into our run, found this to be quite true when we misjudged the rapids here and found our canoe careening sideways, like a an out-of-control car skidding down an icy hill. When we recovered, I jokingly said to Giles, "Only eighteen miles to go."

As it turned out, the river treated us well, although we didn't take it lightly from that point on. We used discretion, pulling out to scout especially tricky spots, and kept our life jackets on, even though we are both strong swimmers and it was a warm June day.

At the next patch of white water we went through the Vs, setting our course to ride the water between boulders. Soon we had our confidence back, and settled back to enjoy the ride. The river relaxed as well, with long stretches of flat water with intermittent rapids that flowed through farm country where grand sycamore trees, with distinctive mottled gray-brown bark, shaded the river. A kingfisher, leaving its perch on a dead branch, flew downstream, calling its displeasure at the two strangers on the river. Floating along, I couldn't help but feel a timelessness to the surrounding hills, rich with new green foliage, so easy on the eye. Seeing a region from a canoe seat gives a unique perspective. Most of the modern-day reminders are out of sight and it's just you, your partner and the river.

I've always felt canoeing is similar to watching a good movie—scenes pass before you, and the longer you watch the more absorbed you become. Soon, curiosity takes over, you wonder what's around the bend, and trips go by all too fast. You become mesmerized by the flowing water, the strokes of the paddle, and the silence. And like a good movie, you love the river and want more.

The Housatonic has been loved by many. Author Chard Powers Smith, in his book, *The Housatonic,* waxed poetic, writing, "The value of a River as a symbol of eternal truth is increased if the valley through which it flows likewise suggested permanence behind change, if the hills are wide and gracious under the sky ... ." And outdoor writer Hal Borland, who knew this country as well as anyone, also saw the permanence and grace of the valley. His bond became so strong he moved to a home on the riverbank. In *This Hill, This Valley,* he chronicles how he made the decision to move here after a serious illness:

"Then I went to the hospital and came back, and it all seemed more of a compromise than a man should make. Reappraisal was inevitable. So we sold our suburban acres and moved to Weatogue, to live, to write, to see and feel and understand a hillside, a river bank, a woodland and valley pasture. I was granted a second chance to know this earth of my origins and I have found here in Weatogue a good vantage point from which to examine it."

Borland's book is a must-read for anyone who forms an attachment to the river. He owned a half mile of river frontage and came to know the Housatonic intimately. Like myself, he felt the timeless quality of the river, writing:

"Here am I, once more dwelling on a river bank, a modern throwback to the company of frogs and salamanders and fish. Whether it is an antediluvian instinct or not which brought me here, I have not yet decided. But I know that my river is a comfort and a satisfaction. It is movement and change in a primal sense, and that movement gives me a sense of permanence. Here I live, planting and harvesting, and there flows the river, fecund and ever changing."

* * * *

Giles and I rode the river, quickly and silently, passing beneath Route 7 at the southern end of Canaan, where pines, maples, white oak and white birch covered gentle hills. Near the river were popples or American aspen, black willows, ash, and I thought I detected the sweet fragrance of the basswood tree's small, creamy white flowers. Clumps of yellow flag grew at the river's edge, with showy yellow flowers on three-foot stalks surrounded by swordlike leaves. A hawk circled lazily overhead, and unseen birds added their song to the murmur of the current. The river was a scene of beauty and tranquillity. Yet it is still recovering from upstream pollution by PCBs which seeped into the river from the General Electric Plant in Pittsfield. And like just about every other river in America, the Housatonic suffered from sewage discharge and dumps located along its banks. Although the tide has turned with passage of the 1972 Clean Water Act, coupled with local action by citizen organizations, the fish in the Housatonic sometimes show traces of the PCBs, and should not be eaten.

Ironically the river is still a first-class fishery. The water is high in nutrients, with a good pH level, primarily from the lime-rock ridge and marble outcrops along its banks. The trout have fast growth rates, and the river bottom is largely composed of small rocks and gravel, so there are plenty of aquatic insects. The river also has strong stewardship by the Housatonic Fly Fishermen's Association (HFFA). In fact, when the PCBs were first discovered in 1980, the state of Connecticut suspended its stocking program, and it was the HFFA which fought to re-establish the fishery. A Trout Management Area with a catch-and-release policy was formed on the river, covering ten miles from the bridge at Routes 7 and 112 downstream to the bridge at Routes 4 and 7. The upper section is open to all forms of fishing, and the lower three and a half miles are for fly-fishing only. Brown trout are the primary fish stocked, but recently rainbows have been added, with both fish producing holdovers over sixteen inches long. Smallmouths, those feisty leapers of pure muscle, also thrive in the river, mixing well with the trout.

I had my fishing rod in the canoe and made several casts, but we were zipping along at a good pace and the offering was not getting down very deep. With such discolored water, I doubt fish could see my streamer unless it floated within a couple inches of them. When the water is high, fish tend to hold near the bottom and out of the current, conserving energy, rather than cruising for food. In normal conditions rainbow trout are often found in the rapids near the center of the river, brook trout in the quiet water at the foot of the rapids where they hide under logs or in the tangle of tree roots, and browns in the deep back eddies or beneath undercut banks. My map showed that we were passing over such celebrated fishing holes as "Push 'em Up Hole," "The Doctor's Hole," and "The Elms," but the water was too high to know where the holes were. Yet two fish showed themselves, enormous bruisers who cleared the water in a leap and landed flat with a loud thwack, like a football hurled into the river. I have no idea what they were, but they made me want to return when the water receded.

Although our angling problem was high water, Housatonic trout have traditionally suffered from high temperatures. During the summer of 1993 there was a fish die off of 80% due to the stress of warm water. Biologists learned that trout, seeking relief near the cool feeder streams, were actually stressed even more by increased water releases from the hydropower dam at Falls Village. Apparently the release of additional warm water was washing right over the cool water refuge at the mouths of the streams. Now, lower flow regimes from the dam have been established for those days when the trout are in danger, and so far it has been a success. The area within 100 feet around the mouths of streams are also off limits to fishing during July and August, and that too has helped the fish survive periods of stress.

* * * *

When Giles and I saw the covered bridge looming ahead we made a beeline to the left bank, beached the canoe and walked up to the bridge. The scene below looked ominous; the river lurched and narrowed, surging through chutes between boulders. I thought of all my valuable camera equipment in the canoe, and walked back to get it, carrying it up to a little shop by the side of the river where Shaker furniture is made. I asked the owner, Ian Ingersoll, if I could leave my equipment with him and pick it up later, explaining that the river was running high and a dunking was not out of the question. He agreed. Giles came into the shop and quickly forgot about the river, enthralled with the craftsmanship of the furniture.

While Giles talked with Ian, I slipped out and went back to the river to do a little fishing. The sun was directly overhead, shining on the water—a poor time to try to lure trout from their lair. But in a relatively quiet seam of water, where the current curled back on itself with flecks of foam, a fish struck. It was a brown trout, and it raced toward the middle of the river, rolled on the surface, then tried to bulldog down. But it was a little guy, and soon was in the net. On the very next cast, a bigger fish hit, a smallmouth bass, clearing the water like a rocket. It too headed for the deeper stretch of river, then jumped again. After a final run it tired, came to the net and I released it.

Hal Borland fished the river, using it as an excuse to be on the water. He would motor upstream a couple miles, then let the current drift his boat back down, catching bass as he went. "I have no notion," wrote Borland, "of telling anyone how to fish. Rivers, as well as fishermen, are insistently individual. And fish—who can read the mind of a fish?" While floating on the river, Borland's eyes, those of an expert naturalist, were usually on the shoreline, noting the trees, shrubs, wild flowers and bird life. He writes that wood ducks are the only ducks he knows of who perch in trees, and how mergansers will sometimes nest in trees just like the wood duck. His favorite time of year to be on the river is October:

"The sky is deep blue; the wine of swamp maples and amber of popple are spilled in vast reflections, like pigment floating on the water. October is the time to make a long, leisurely trip on any river if you would know how beautiful it can be. Then the Autumn rains come, bringing down the leaves and the river flows with a variegation of color that is unbelievable."

Reading Borland's book, *Beyond Your Doorstep,* is pure delight and one of the most entertaining ways to make yourself a self-taught naturalist.

* * * *

When Giles returned to the canoe we both decided that discretion is the better part of valor, and we portaged around the bridge abutments and huge waves, putting in just a few feet downstream of the bridge. Without the camera equipment in the canoe, I felt a new sense of freedom, knowing that if we capsized it's no big deal. We attacked the rapids with new zeal, hooting and hollering while barreling through chutes, having near misses with boulders, and threading the needle between a log and rock.

On the east bank of the river were railroad tracks and just beyond the land rose sharply at Mine Mountain. My topographical map showed this ridge running north–south as a compression of brown contour indicating its dramatic rise. In fact the entire eastern shoreline looked like a wild place, covered with dark, sweeping hemlocks, beckoning us to beach our canoe and enter the forest. And where the river pulled away from Route 7, I thought that I'd like to come back in the autumn when the water's down, and wade the river in an old pair of sneakers to fish the pockets inaccessible to most anglers.

A sign at the Falls Village rest area where we launched warned of a ledge downstream from the covered bridge. The sign said:

YOU WILL HEAR THE ROAR,

BUT IT IS HARD TO SEE AT HIGH WATER

We neither saw it nor heard it until we were just a few feet away.

Giles was in the bow, and he later said it looked like the waves would swallow the canoe when it pitched over the ledge. The drop was only about a foot, but the angry waves seemed to curl back on themselves, and it was clearly a dangerous spot. The river smacked the canoe menacingly and threw spray over the bow, as if to remind us who was boss.

(Small falls in a river with large volumes of water create dangerous hydraulics when the force of the water drops to the bottom of the river, rushes along the bottom, then rises and rushes back upstream to fill the void. This is called a reversal, where the water is circulating like a vertical wheel. When in doubt about conditions and your abilities, avoid canoeing on stretches of river where these ledges and reversals exist.)

Fortunately we shot through without incident. But even in normal conditions canoeists get into trouble at this spot and other rocky stretches downstream. A woman from Cornwall, who runs a B&B, told me story about one of her guests who ran the river here:

"There are dozens of wallets and keys at the bottom of the river. One guest was going in July so I gave him a big horse pin to pin his keys to his bathing suit so he wouldn't loose them. Well, they capsized and he came back with only a towel around his waist. Claims he lost his keys *and* his bathing suit when he went over."

She also told me that rocks protruding during low water frequently mean getting out and walking the canoe around obstructions. Giles and I only saw a few boulder tops, and it was hard to imagine the river as a series of shallow riffles, especially the way we literally flew around a bend just beyond the ledge.

(Water thrown to an outside of a bend will be deeper and faster. Bends in the river are another spot where canoeists get in trouble because the current will sweep them to the outside bend where there might be fallen trees—a dangerous hazard, where the current can pin you and your canoe against the trees. Hug the inside shoreline until you can see that the outside is free from hazards.)

At two popular fishing holes, we encountered the first anglers we'd seen all day. We spoke with one, and he too had had little luck, but said he just wanted to spend time on the water. Who could blame him? The sun was shining, the breeze was gentle, and birds were singing, after the prior two days of storms. Just like the trapper who gets cabin fever in the winter, the angler we met had, I suspect, "civilization fever" caused by being indoors too long.

These days it's almost a health hazard to be inside so much, yet many of us stay there willingly. The simple sport of trout fishing or canoeing a river is to step back into the elemental world from which we came, to which we belong, but which, I'm afraid, too many of us have forgot. Or perhaps even worse, some of us take the electronic world with us into the rivers, forests and mountains, calling home on cell phones to let someone at home know "how beautiful it really is."

* * * *

As we approached Kent we passed a few "pillows" of water that covered submerged boulders, and a stretch of rapids, but generally had a nice run of flat water with intermittent riffles until the end of the trip. During one long stretch of calm water we ate lunch and only used the paddles for steering, watching an osprey wing its way upstream. Here the river is dotted with islands, and again I thought of all the fishing opportunities during normal water conditions. Who knows what size of brown trout lurk in the depths of the river far from the road?

We began planning our next trip. Rivers lead to adventure, and every time I make a voyage I ask myself why I don't do it more often. I never tire of flowing water. Every trip is a fresh experience, a new little wonder revealing itself. Even Thoreau, who spent countless hours on his beloved Concord and Sudbury Rivers, never lost the thrill. Writing in his Journal on September 5th, 1838, he marveled:

"For the first time it occurred to me this afternoon what a piece of wonder a river is. A huge volume of matter ceaselessly rolling through the fields and meadows of this substantial earth—making haste from the high places ... ."

A river, especially one that you float on again and again, can possess you like few other things on earth.

EXPLORER'S NOTES
Recommended reading

Hal Borland's several books about living in the country along the Housatonic are all first-class works of nature writing. Among my favorites are *This Hill, This Valley,* and *Beyond Your Doorstep.*

Canoeing Massachusetts, Rhode Island and Connecticut, by Ken Weber, is an excellent guidebook.

The AMC River Guide: Massachusetts, Connecticut and Rhode Island, gives a summary of what to expect on all major rivers in these states.

Campgrounds

Situated on the banks of the river is the state-run Housatonic Meadows Campground (860-672-6772).

Fishing on the river

Late May and June as well as autumn is the best time to fish the river. Because the trout see quite a few anglers they can be picky, and as a general rule fly-fishermen do better with small flies when the action is slow, or working a nymph deep. You should be aware that the river level fluctuates due to releases at the dam, and you can call Northeast Utilities for a taped message of flow times for Falls Village (203-824-7861). Take caution when wading, and you should keep an eye on a rock in the river to see if the water level has risen above it. If so, head for the banks. Fishing licenses can be purchased at Clarke Outdoors. The Housatonic Fly Fishermen's Association sells a map and guide called *Fishing the Housatonic River Trout*

Management Area for $7.50 which includes postage. Send checks to HFFA at P.O. Box 5092, Hamden, CT 06518.

Canoeing

Clarke Outdoors is located on Route 7 in West Cornwall, offering canoe and kayak rentals, white-water rafting in the spring, and instructions for beginners all the way to white-water experts (860-672-6365). Riverrunning Expeditions in Falls Village also rents canoes.

Our trip was unusual for June because of extremely high water due to a wet spring and recent thunderstorms. Some of the river, in normal summer conditions, is usually filled with exposed rocks which will scrape your canoe and challenge your maneuvering skills.

The Housatonic during high-water conditions is a dangerous river. It's best first to check conditions with a local outfitter before starting out, and consider taking a canoe training and safety course. Try and time your trip when the water is not too high and not too low, which allows for some of the best canoeing in New England.

The International River Classification System rates rapids is as follows:

Class I—Moving water with few riffles and small waves. Few or no obstructions.

Class II—Easy rapids with waves up to three feet, and wide, clear channels that are obvious without scouting. Some maneuvering is required.

Class III—Rapids with high, irregular waves often capable of swamping an open canoe. Narrow passages that often require complex maneuvering. May require scouting from shore.

Class IV—Long, difficult rapids with constricted passages that often require precise maneuvering in very turbulent waters. Scouting from shore is necessary and conditions make rescue difficult. Generally not possible for open canoes.

Class V—Extremely difficult, long and very violent rapids with highly congested routes, which always should be scouted from shore. Rescue conditions are difficult, and there is significant hazard to life in the event of a mishap.

Class VI—Difficulties of Class V carried to the extreme of navigability. Nearly impossible and very dangerous. For teams of experts only after close study and with all precautions taken.

Visit the library and read books on canoe safety before starting any trip. A good instruction book will tell you how to read the river, paddling maneuvers, and what to do if you capsize.

(The main thing to remember if you capsize in rapids is to stay upstream of your canoe to avoid being pinned between it and an obstacle. And never stand up in fast water. Even if the river is only thigh deep, your foot could become wedged in rocks and the water's force can hold you completely submerged. You should float on your back with your feet downstream on the surface to so you can see where you are going and push off rocks with your feet. Read an instructional book and take a safety course to learn the complete set of skills for canoeing high water.)

Exploring

At Kent Falls State Park, Kent Falls Brook cascades over a rocky hillside on the way to the river. A short, steep trail will bring you to the top.

The peaks of Pine Knob offer great river views. Hiking trials are located about one mile north of the village of Cornwall Bridge at a parking area on Route 7.

The covered bridge at West Cornwall was built in 1864 using a lattice truss design patented by Itheil Town of New Haven.

Bulls Covered Bridge is located in Kent, with a recreation area on the west bank of the river.

The Sloane Stanley Museum in Kent has early-American tools and implements donated by Eric Sloane, a writer and artist who had a love of history and craftsmanship. Be sure to check out the book he illustrated and edited, *Diary of an Early American Boy*, sold in the museum. The remains of the Kent Iron Furnace, built in 1826, are behind the museum, as is a reproduction of a seventeenth-century cabin.

The town of Sharon has a handsome green, laid out in 1739, with well-preserved eighteenth-century homes around it and an unusual clock tower with a working clock in it.

Salisbury, known as the arsenal of the America Revolution for its many metal-working furnaces, is another town with a center of uncommon beauty. Not far from the town center is Bald Peak and Mount Riga, offering good hiking and views.

If time permits, follow the river north into Massachusetts, where a number of special places await discovery. Bartholomews Cobble, in Ashley Falls, is a riverside reservation owned by the Trustees of Reservations, with many rare and unusual plants growing among the marble outcrops.

The Ice Glen, just south of the center of Stockbridge, has a boulder-filled chasm and old-growth pine trees. A foot bridge spans the river at the End of Park Street, just off Route 7.

Litchfield Hills Travel Council (860-567-4506).

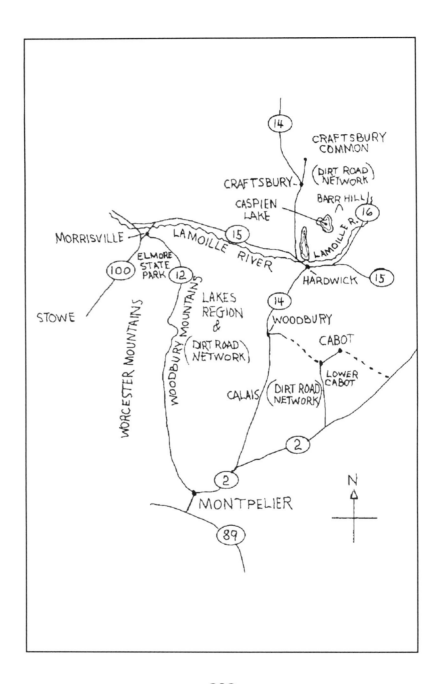

A Cabin in the Mountains—
the Rough Country
of North Central Vermont

From the cabin's porch above the pond I can see miles to the west. Woodbury Mountain, Hobart Mountain and dozens of unnamed hills stretch darkly on the horizon. Although the only water in view is the pond directly below, there must be at least twenty-five ponds and lakes within a four-mile radius. A few cabins and homes are tucked away in hollows and along lake shores, but for the most part the land is forest.

Two mountain ranges, the Woodbury Mountains and the Worcester Mountains, separate this rough and isolated country from the tourist mecca of Stowe, Vermont. As the crow flies, my cabin is only fourteen miles east of Stowe Village, but there are no nearby east–west roads that penetrate the mountains, so Stowe is over an hour away by car. There are no golf courses or ski areas close by, and the roads are mostly dirt, often turning into quagmires during mud season. Some might see this isolation as a liability for owning land in the country, but for me it is a blessing. While real estate values are sky-high in Stowe, here the prices are considerably less, allowing me to buy these few acres some twenty years ago.

For the most part, development has stayed clear of my cabin and the surrounding towns of Calais, Worcester, Elmore,

Woodbury and Cabot, leaving the region a perfect place for back-road rambles. The fishing's not bad either. Most of the larger lakes have smallmouth bass and trout, and the ponds usually have smallmouth and pickerel. To the north is the Lamoille River, with brook trout in the upper reaches and rainbow and brown trout in its mid-section, some of legendary size.

Tonight, a cool evening in early May, I sit alone on the porch, dressed warmly in a down jacket and hat, sipping a beer. I've been here for two days, taking full advantage of the awakening land before the black flies claim it for their own. My atlas is spread before me, and I study the roads leading to Cabot, trying to retrace the route I followed earlier in the day. It's funny how you think you know a place, then you poke around in a new direction, finding scenery that makes you stare in awe. Cabot Plains did that to me.

Located just three miles to the northeast of Cabot Center, Cabot Plains sits high on a hill, where pastures of lush green grass and wild flowers provide the open space for panoramic vistas. When I visited, a storm had just passed, and the sun occasionally broke out from behind gray clouds, making for incredible contrasts of light and dark. While the hilltop directly in front of me was glistening in light, more distant hills were dim and brooding in a purple-gray hue. Then the clouds would shift a bit, bathing the farm in the valley below in sunshine, while the foreground was gloomy with gray shadows.

The dramatic skies were the perfect backdrop for the forlorn hilltop cemetery of Cabot Plains. Surrounded by a white rail fence, with a wooden arch above the entrance, the cemetery lies along the path of the Bayley-Hazen Military Road. The road dates back to the Revolution, when George Washington ordered its construction to serve as a military route connecting the upper Connecticut River to Saint Francis, Quebec. Not unlike current government projects, the road was never completed, because General Washington soon realized the road that could carry his Patriot army northward could also be used by the English to come south. And so the passage never made it to Canada, instead stopping at Lowell, Vermont, about thirty miles north. Today the road is little more than a footpath in places, but it gets me dreaming about walking its entire length some day.

As beautiful as the view from Cabot Plain was that day, I'll remember what happened next in much more vivid detail. On my way back to the cabin, my eye caught a new logging road, and I decided to explore it by foot. The road angled up a ridge, passing beneath huge hemlocks and white birch. A fresh and pleasing smell of earth, ferns and evergreen filled the air, making the walk pure pleasure.

As I walked deeper into the woods, I flushed a partridge, stopping me in my tracks, startling me out of my trance and bringing my mind back to the trail at hand. Up ahead was the logging field I suspected I'd find, and the road curled around its edge leading to an overlook.

I always carry a day pack with me into the woods, and I found a dry place in the sun to sit and eat a snack. Below me the logging field stretched down the hill, stumps and debris scattered about the clearing, and logs neatly stacked at the far end. I must have been sitting there for five minutes before I noticed the bear.

It was about a hundred feet away, going about its business digging at a stump, then rolling over a log. The bear must have been upwind, because it had no idea that I was there.

It's one thing to see an animal this large while passing in a car, but quite another to see it while sitting alone in the woods. I'm not ashamed to admit to a rush of fear. Bear, springtime ... cubs? I didn't realize at the time that a bear this large could only be a male, and my eyes searched the logging field for signs of cubs. After satisfying myself that there were none, I relaxed and watched the show, mesmerized, thinking how incredible it is that something this big still lives wild and free.

The bear's strength was evident in the way it pushed aside a log about a foot in diameter with its paw. Then it put its nose to the ground, perhaps to lick up grubs or insects. It continued this digging, pushing and licking, all the while inching closer to where I sat. This was the first black bear I'd ever come across in the woods, and I wanted to stretch the experience until it noticed or smelled me. But I began to get uncomfortable, the closer it came. I'd estimate it weighed 400 pounds.

I decided I'd seen enough, but wondered how to scare it off. First, I gave a short whistle to see what he would do. Instead of running, he immediately stood straight up on hind legs, searching and scanning with eyes, ears and nose. His head, now that he was directly facing me, was truly enormous.

I didn't move a muscle, and the bear still didn't locate me on the ridge above. Seconds passed, and I decided it best to let him know exactly where I was, so I clapped my hands together. In a split second the bear was on all fours charging away into the woods. I'll never forget the crashing sounds which rang out as he smashed through brush and trees. And then, just as suddenly as it started, the noise ceased. Although I couldn't see the bear, it sounded like he had stopped somewhere near the lower part of the logging road—the same stretch I'd have to descend. And by now it was almost dark.

As I walked down the path, everything before me looked like a bear. The stump in the woods was a hunched-over bear, a log in the shadows was a bear lying in wait, and a tall shadow directly to the side of the path caused me to hold my breath, appearing to be exactly like a bear on its hind legs.

Looking back at the incident from the comfort of my cabin porch, its easy to laugh at the way I sang as I went down the trail, hoping the bear would hear me long before I came anywhere near him in the twilight. I'll never know if the strategy actually helped move the bear on, but I never saw him again.

According to the Vermont Fish and Game Department, there are probably more bears in the state now than at any time during the past 200 years. This is primarily due to reforestation, after the early settlers had cleared an amazing three quarters of the state. Today, over eighty percent of Vermont's countryside is forested, and the bear population is flourishing. Vermont is also farsighted enough to have passed Act 250, which protects crucial wildlife habitats, including wildlife corridors and oak and beech groves frequented by bears.

The black bear is found in just about every state in America except Rhode Island, New Jersey and Kansas. Here in the east, Maine has the largest population of them, with more than 20,000 bears roaming the forests. But seeing a bear is not an everyday occurrence, because they are shy and reclusive. Solitary creatures, they travel alone, unless the mother has cubs, or when adult males and females get together to mate in June or July. Cubs are born in the winter, and the usual number of offspring is one the first time, and two thereafter. They leave the den after about three months, and stay with the mother until their second summer.

In the South, bears den up for only a few days at a time in the winter; in the North the period of inactivity lasts from about November to April. This is often called hibernation, yet it is not the true hibernation of such animals as the woodchuck, whose body temperature drops dramatically—the bear's temperature drops only a few degrees. Black bears can be aroused from a winter's nap in a matter of minutes, and if they feel threatened they will charge out of the den. But during a typical winter, the bear stays in slumber—unless giving birth—not eating, drinking, defecating or urinating. The den may be a cave or ledge, windfalls, or merely the side of a large fallen tree. The females tend to be a bit more selective in choosing a site than the males.

When bears emerge from their dens in the spring, they are ravenous, working hard to find food, such as honey from bee-hives, rodents, grasses and clovers, and the new leaves of aspen and maple. Berries become the primary food when summer and fall come, supplemented by nuts and apples. Beechnuts are their most important food in the fall when they fattening for winter, and beech trees are a good place to see bear sign. Look on the beech tree's smooth gray bark for claw marks made when the bear either climbed or clawed the tree. Black bears will also make "nests" in beech trees, where they stack up broken branches to rest on. You may also see evidence of bear digs in a beech grove, where the ground will be churned up by the bears as they grub for fallen nuts beneath the leaves.

Black bears can climb, swim, and as I found out, even stand on their hind legs (rising to almost six feet). Bears can be extremely quick while running, climbing trees or taking a swipe at something. They would rather avoid than confront humans, and mauling has been extremely rare, with fewer than thirty people killed by black bears in the United States in the last century.

Trouble does start, however, when people feed bears or when bears learn that areas habitated by humans contain food (such as in trash barrels), which can make them into a nuisance or worse. Campers have been terrified by aggressive bears that stay close to a campsite because they smell food. Never leave food out in the open (or the remains of fish you might have cleaned), but instead seal them, and if camping near the car put the food inside. If camping in the back country, string the sealed food high up in trees far from the campsite, and be sure the tree branch cannot support a bear. Don't sleep in the clothes you cooked in, and never take food into a tent.

* * * *

Now, as I sit on the porch and watch the last streaks of pink fade over the western hills, I think of all the nights I slept under the stars rather than in the cabin—and I think of the bear. Maybe tonight I'll compromise and sleep on the porch.

It's funny how your comfort level changes in relationship to time spent in the woods. When I first bought the cabin I'd only come up with friends, finding the seclusion and utter quiet too lonely to spend the weekend by myself. Later I'd spend an occasional solitary weekend there, sleeping in the cabin, locking the door and waking frequently. The transition from suburbia with all its background noise and people to this isolated hilltop was so drastic, I'd be uncomfortable the first night. How odd that the lack of noise would seem strange rather than soothing. But with age comes wisdom and comfort in being alone, and now, I look forward to solitary trips, finding it a time of renewal. I never sleep in the cabin, but on the porch, or occasionally outside on a tarp where I can lie back and see the stars through the opening in the trees. I once told a friend that my best night's sleep now come when I simply take my tarp and sleeping bag and curl up in the woods. He said "don't tell anybody; sounds too weird."

I've never been bothered by animals in the woods, although I've heard plenty. And I've never been bothered by people I meet in the woods, even the hunters who use my land. I don't post my property, and believe other out-of-staters should not post theirs. It's wrong when property rights crowd out freedom of movement. Hikers should be able to travel through, hunters to hunt in season, and berry pickers should pick away. As soon as landowners begin to feel that the land is their little kingdom to do as they please, they pull themselves away from nature, spoiling it for others in the process. Far better to look at the land you own as temporarily in your care, and focus on the land itself rather than on ownership.

We should all have an acre we know intimately, whether we own it or not. It would be a life-long project to learn the name of every plant and tree that grows on it, to understand its seasonal transformations, to grow closer and closer to the earth with each passing year. Only through time and quiet observation would it unlock its secrets. Follow a game trail, sit quietly against a tree and watch dawn awaken your special place, or study a brook with the eye of a child.

* * * *

I drag a mattress onto the porch, put on my ski hat and down jacket, then curl up in my sleeping bag. Below, by the pond, an owl hoots, then all is silent. Cool air and warm body make for the best sleeping conditions, and I drift off.

When the light wakes me about seven the next morning, I make a quick cup of coffee, and sit out on the deck with my atlas and maps spread before me. So many places to hike. The Worcester Mountain Range to the west in Elmore is as wild and rugged as any rough country in New England, as are the steep ridges of the Woodbury Mountains. But a spot to the north has caught my attention—Barr Hill. My brother Mark, who lives nearby, told me of the spectacular vistas from the hillside, and I wondered how I missed it all these years. I hop in the car and head toward Greensboro.

But first breakfast. I decide to treat myself, driving to Hardwick and loading up on mega calories at the Village Café. The coffee is served in thick white mugs, and the banana-walnut pancakes are rich and tasty. I can look out the window and see a stretch of rapids on the Lamoille River. After the meal, I walk out on a suspension bridge above the river just behind the restaurant, and wonder if anglers pass up this stretch of river because it's in the heart of town. I make a mental note to give it a try—there are plenty of dark recesses under the rocks for rainbows to hide.

Rather than take the back roads direct to Barr Hill, I follow Route 14 north past cigar-shaped Eligo Pond and the surrounding marshes and beaver ponds to Craftsbury Common, one of Vermont's most charming town greens. It's a large, square common, completely open in the middle, circled by maples and a white rail fence. Simple homes, all painted white, grace the outside of the common, and a tall bandstand rises from the far corner. There is no one on the common; in fact there is no sign of life. I recall a picnic I once had here with my new girlfriend, now my wife, wanting to show her the charming side of Vermont's Northeast Kingdom, rather than its ruggedness and isolation. It was an autumn day, with orange splashes of color on the maples lining the white fence, and a friendly Irish setter joined us for the picnic.

Craftsbury also brings back a different kind of memory, one of strange apparitions in the woods. In 1994 a Massachusetts man was visiting his mother and grandmother here when he went up a hillside, had a smoke and saw three brown forms glide through the woods. He assumed they were deer until they skirted a swamp and came into full view. Not believing what was just 100 feet in front of him, he rubbed his eyes and refocused. Then he ran like hell back to his house, and called biologists at the Vermont Fish and Wildlife Department to report mountain lions. One biologist, who had interviewed several other people claiming they saw catamounts, rushed to the scene with tracking experts, hopeful of gathering evidence, since the sighting had just happened.

They quickly found the tracks, following them along the forested ridges for miles. Just as they were about to give up, unusual-looking scat was sighted on the trail, which they scraped into a plastic bag and later sent to the U.S. Fish and Wildlife Service forensic lab in Oregon. The scat was analyzed and the finding was conclusive—mountain lion. And if there are three confirmed cats in Craftsbury, it's a good bet there are more scattered throughout the Northeast Kingdom.

* * * *

From Craftsbury I head south, passing the eastern shore of Caspian Lake, a deep, icy-cold body of water formed by two glacial scoops meeting in the middle, home now to salmon and lake trout. Then up the dirt roads to Barr Hill. The roads get progressively worse, and I hit a washout, hiking the last half mile to the trail head. But I'm glad I'm on foot: this last section of road passes through open meadow interspersed with spruce and fir, with a new view of purple-blue mountains appearing with each passing step. Juniper and wild flowers dot the meadow, and veins of quartz twinkle in the sun. I walk around the hilltop on a looping trail, picking a sprig of fir and inhaling its crushed needles from time to time. The hill is in the "mixing zone" where deciduous trees such as sugar maple, beech and yellow birch grow alongside the boreal conifers of white spruce, red spruce, balsam fir and northern white cedar. Moss carpets the forest floor, shining iridescent green where dappled sunlight strikes it.

When I complete the loop I sit in the meadow, soaking in the sun and the south-southwestern vista. In the distance are the faint outlines of Camel's Hump, Mount Mansfield and

Madonna Peak, all of which have given me great hikes. But it's the hills in the foreground that hold my eyes—Woodbury Mountain, Mount Hunger and Elmore Mountain—the mountains I've come to know from countless trips to the cabin. I think of all the tramps I've taken in those forests, think of the friends I've spent weekends with roaming the hills, and give thanks for the simple things that mean so much.

EXPLORER'S NOTES

The *Vermont Atlas and Gazetteer* produced by DeLorme Mapping is the best source for finding the network of dirt roads that crisscross the north central Vermont region. Using this atlas or the U. S. Geological Survey maps make exploration infinitely more enjoyable. The Mount Worcester 7.5 quadrangle details the rugged hills of Worcester and Elmore, where Putnam State Forest is located, and the Plainfield 15-minute series quadrangle includes Woodbury and Cabot.

Barr Hill is located a couple miles to the northeast of Caspian Lake. From the public beach on Caspian Lake take a left past the general store, bear right at the next fork, and then left at the next fork which goes up Barr Hill Road. Stay on this road until you see the sign for Barr Hill Nature Preserve.

Hardwick Chamber of Commerce (802-472-5006).

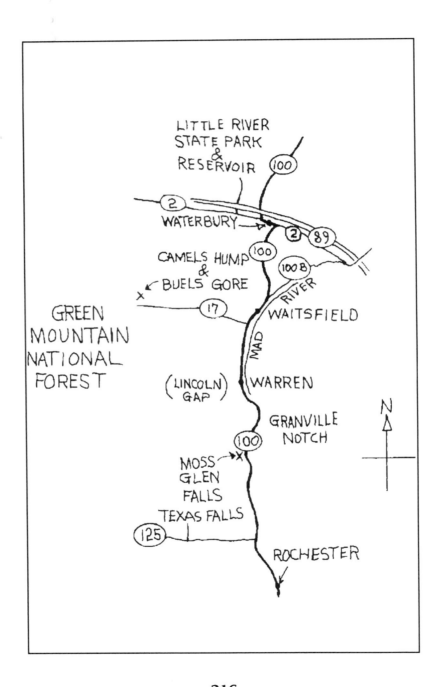

Kids, Goshawks and Abandoned Towns— A Slice of Route 100

Clear water dashes over a bar of gravel, then curls into a deep pool at the base of a twenty-foot-tall ledge of granite. The perfect swimming hole. My kids, age eight and five, climb to the top of the ledge, peer over the edge and stop. I expect them, or at least the younger one, to turn around, but instead they step back and take a running leap, catching me off guard as I wait in the pool below. When they surface next to me they look surprised at how deep they knifed into the cool water, then break into huge grins.

Is there anything better than a refreshing dip in a mountain river in August? It's one of the reasons summer is my favorite season in Vermont—work up a sweat, from biking, hiking or fishing, and there is always a nearby swimming hole to invigorate and rejuvenate. Here along Route 100 in greater Waitsfield, the Mad River offers numerous pools of water, perfect for swimming in the afternoon, or drifting a fly in the morning or evening.

Introducing children to the natural world takes patience and knowing their limits. A hike with a child can be a wonderful bonding adventure or a total nightmare. More than once I've overestimated their endurance, watching them bound up a hillside, only to have them flag near the summit, with you-know-who carrying them back down. And so on this weekend ramble, with just me and the two kids, I try to keep the activity moderate, and let them plan some of the excursions. We would spend one night at my rustic (no plumbing) cabin, but tonight would be a real treat; lodging at the Lareau Farm Country Inn, conveniently located on the opposite side of Route 100 from our favorite swimming hole.

The inn and farm date back to 1832, and the now-restored inn has fourteen guest rooms. The atmosphere is relaxed and casual, and my kids fall in love with the family dog, walking with it out back to see the horses. No inn is complete without a country porch, and the Lareau Farm has a wrap-around affair, where one can sit in a rocker and gaze out at the Green Mountains. In the morning breakfast is served on the back side of the porch, where the appetite grows keen in the country air and sunshine.

* * * *

After I put the kids to bed, I walk through the meadow down to the river and watch the delicate rings of rising trout, thinking that it would take years of exploration to discover all the backwoods destinations along Route 100, which runs north–south through the center of the state. Vermont's Long Trail roughly parallels this section of Route 100 and can be reached by driving through Lincoln Gap.

The Lincoln Gap Road goes through Vermont's steepest pass and also its highest at 2,424 feet, crossing the Long Trail near the border of the towns of Warren and Lincoln. By hiking south on the Long Trail about thirty minutes from Lincoln

Gap one finds a ledge with tremendous western views. Called "Sunset Rock," it's a great hiking destination in the late afternoon, but don't get trapped on the trail when dusk falls. A more strenuous hike northward from the gap leads to the summit of Mount Abraham which supports a community of fragile alpine-tundra vegetation. Although the mountain is only 2.6 miles from the Lincoln Gap Road, the trail is steep, so allow plenty of time for the hike. There are fine views from the summit. Ambitious climbers often try a ten-mile gap-to-gap hike on the Long Trail, starting at Lincoln Gap and ending northward at the Appalachian Gap, passing seven summits of roughly 4,000 feet.

Just off Route 100 in Granville is Moss Glen Falls, located in a chasm at Granville Gulch. Driving through the Gulch gives you a taste of the vastness of the Green Mountain National Forest, and you might see a moose coming down off the hills to feed in the wetlands along the road. Farther south and a couple miles west on Route 125 is Texas Falls Recreation Area, where the waterfall has carved out flumes and potholes, and a trail follows Hancock Brook.

For poking about back roads you can't beat the country lanes just to the east of Route 100 in Warren and Waitsfield. The looping road that cuts through the village of Warren passes by an unusual mixture of homes, each different from the next, ranging from designs by well-known architects to handyman specials. There's an 1880 covered bridge, and nearby is the Warren Country Store, a former stagecoach inn on the banks of the river. It's a good place to stop for lunch and eat on the deck above the river.

From Warren Village you can take Brook Road to East Warren Road, which runs north into the farm country and plateaus above Waitsfield, offering the kind of scenery that sets Vermont apart from every other state in the Union. Besides the sweeping vistas, the road takes you past a unique round barn and two more covered bridges. Vermont has its own mystique because it has preserved its heritage better than any other New England state. Maybe that's why in 1993 the National Trust for Historic Preservation placed the entire state on its list of endangered places. The whole state, from the border with the Berkshires to Canadian line, has beauty worth protecting.

* * * *

When we left Waitsfield the next morning we followed Route 100 north to Waterbury and the Little River State Park. The access road to the park winds along the Little River (known for its rainbow trout) to the dam at the southern end of the Water- bury Reservoir, where the fishing is especially good. But with two young children, I came not for the fishing but rather for a hike up into an abandoned town on Ricker Mountain.

In the mid-1800s there were a number of farms scattered on the hill, with school, cemeteries and a sawmill. As happened to other hilltop communities, the flatter, richer and free lands out west drew its residents away from grubbing out a living on the steep, rocky soil of New England, and by the 1920s the community was a ghost town.

Forest has reclaimed the land, but the foundations, ceme- tery, and signs of the mill remain. On the Dalley Loop Trail one farmhouse, the Almeron Goodell House, is still standing, and that's where we head. As we walk the old road, I tried to picture rolling farm fields and horse-drawn carriages bouncing down the road, but the silence of the forest makes the leap of imagination difficult.

The hike to the farmhouse was memorable for three reasons. The first is that it marked a turning point in my eight-year-old daughter's interest in hiking. Prior to the trip we had spent many a father/daughter weekend together, hiking all day then spending the night at a B&B. But now the hiking part was "boring" to her, even though walking to an abandoned home (I told her it was haunted) was usually the kind of adventure kids love. I suspect I'll loose her as a hiking companion until her teenage years are almost over, but I'm hoping I've planted the seed for outdoor activities, and that it only lies dormant until a later time.

My son enjoyed the hike, but not his "pet." He had found a large grasshopper, still torpid from the night's cool air. He placed it on his shoulder and it stayed there as he climbed the mountain. Occasionally he would talk to it, giving it an encouraging word so it wouldn't be scared of the "haunted house." But halfway into the hike Brian let out a scream, and I turned to see him pointing at his neck, sobbing. It seems his new friend regained its energy and turned on its host and master, crawling from his shoulder to his neck where it bit or tweezed him, or whatever grasshoppers do when they no longer want to play.

The other significant event on the hike was the sight of a goshawk, an uncommon hawk, large enough to prey on squirrel, snowshoe hare and grouse. Recognized by the broad white eye stripe and chilling, high-pitched "kak" calls, the hawk sat in a tree, staring at us as we climbed the hill. It gave us what looked like the evil eye, then let out a scream before taking wing, navigating effortlessly at a high rate of speed beneath the forest canopy.

If it were a few weeks earlier in the season I would have suspected the hawk might have a nest nearby—and I would have ducked for cover, as they are fierce defenders of their nesting area. They give fair warning with their cries of alarm, and then attack, swooping down and raking a victim's head with their talons. The female, the more aggressive sex, is larger than the male, with a wing span of four feet—enough to intimidate most creatures that get too close to the nest. They are woodland birds, seldom seen, preferring secluded mixed woodlands, like the forest at Little River State Park.

The goshawk only added to the eerie feeling of the abandoned settlement of Ricker Mountain, and the weathered old Goodell farmhouse fit the mood perfectly. Set on the side of a knoll, the home is of brown hewed timbers and hand-split gray shingles, with a couple of gnarled old apple trees growing in the small yard. We picnicked out front by the goldenrod and queen anne's lace, and I wondered when the forest would swallow up this house like the others, hiding the scars, returning the mountain to its original wildness.

EXPLORER'S NOTES

The Route 100 area

The Little River State Park is located in the Ricker Block of Mount Mansfield State Forest, which encompasses more than 37,000 acres. Besides miles of hiking trails, fishing, swimming and boating in Waterbury Reservoir, it offers great camping facilities. For information, maps and tour guides, write to the Park Ranger at Little River State Park, RD 1, Waterbury, VT 05676.

Encompassing more than 350,000 acres, the Green Mountain National Forest totals at least five percent of Vermont's land surface, straddling the ridge line of Vermont's major mountain range. Wilderness camping is allowed in certain sections. For information write to the Public Affairs Director at 231 North Main St, Rutland, VT 05701 or call 802-747-6765. To contact the Rochester Ranger District, call 802-767-4261.

The Lareau Farm Country Inn in Waitsfield is owned and operated by Dan and Susan Easley (802-496-4949).

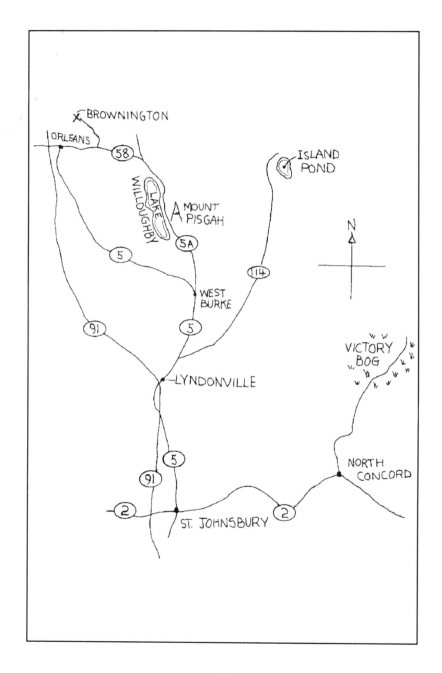

Into the Kingdom—Lake Willoughby, Mount Pisgah, Victory Bog and Beyond

The odd shape of the mountain is what made me climb it when reason said to save the hike for another day.

Mount Pisgah looks like half of it has been sheared away, as if the glaciers concentrated all their power here, scouring the land with a grinding force beyond imagination. Thousand-foot-high granite cliffs rise dramatically from the steely waters of Lake Willoughby, disappearing in the dark clouds near the mountain's summit. If the view from below was this incredible I could only imagine what it was from the top.

Normally the climb should take about an hour, but freshets cascade down the trail, making the rocks slick, and I pick my way carefully along the trail. It's May 4, and I'm well ahead of black-fly season and apparently ahead of spring as well. A few patches of snow cling stubbornly to low-lying depressions and the wind still has winter's bite. The trees are bare, and the forest looks like a black-and-white picture, highlighted here and there with brown hues.

The trail switches back, then begins a more gradual ascent along the spine of the mountain. Soon I'm at Pulpit Rock, a granite outcrop that juts toward the lake with a sheer drop of about 500 feet. I sit at the edge of the cliff and marvel at the

scene. Willoughby stretches out below, long and narrow, locked
in on the east by Mount Pisgah and on the west by Mount
Hor. It's said that the lake reminds people of the fjords of Nor-
way and from this vantage point that's exactly what I thought.
With clouds partially shrouding the surrounding mountains,
and the lake a slate gray, the whole scene was a haunting one,
giving me the feeling of aloneness. Nothing stirred on the
mountain, and nothing stirred below; all living things were still
in their dens, nests, burrows or homes.

Open heights have always made me uncomfortable, and
this one is no exception, giving me a touch of vertigo. So
instead of standing, I slide off the rock on my backside, so as
not to risk rising suddenly and becoming dizzy. Why is it, I
wonder, that I enjoy riding in airplanes (even going up in a
glider once), when exposed ledges like this get under my skin?

Still more climbing ahead. Sprinkles of raindrops patter on
dry leaves and a western breeze rocks the treetops. The silence is
broken by the cry of a raven, circling alone just above the trees.
At least something else is alive up here, but ravens, like turkey
vultures, remind me of Poe's dark lines rather than the glories
of nature.

I'm sweating heavily now, despite an air temperature in the
thirties. Another half hour of climbing brings me to a grove of
white birch mixed with spruce and fir, and I rest on a log, taking a long pull of water from my bottle. Crushing a sprig of
spruce in my hand, I breath deeply of the pungent evergreen,
gathering strength from the scent, savoring the smell of the
north country.

Back on my feet the trail gets narrower, pulling away from the lake. More snow in the gullies, more softwoods. I've read that arctic plants, such as sweet broom and mountain saxifrage, grow on the cliffs, and I believe it—the temperature seems to drop every five minutes. I look at my watch—3:30. Just enough time for a dash to the summit and then down before dark. But there's five inches of snow on the trail now, and mine are the only footsteps. I pass an exposed area of bedrock with a view of Burke Mountain, but it's not the northern panorama I'm after.

I know I'm close to summit, know I'm just minutes away from one of Vermont's best views, but I can't find the trail. There is heavy, icy snow everywhere, some pockets rising to my knees. I *think* I know which direction the Upper Overlook is, but what if I'm wrong? I pause, debating my options. If I get lost or twist an ankle, no one knows I'm here. Ten or twenty years ago I might have pushed on a bit farther, probably achieved my goal, and probably would have been perfectly safe. But probably is no guarantee, so I wait some more and think.

Taking time to assess a situation *before* you plod ahead is wisdom. For me, that wisdom comes from spending so much time in the woods (which brings respect), age (I've crossed the forty mark), and a couple of close calls in the past (a mishap on a Vermont river and a brief period of being lost in northern Maine). There is really no decision to make. Only a fool would take a risk here. I'm tired, it's approaching dusk, and the temperatures are at levels where hypothermia could kill me before the night's over. Making the wrong decision, because of the siren call of the summit, is what gets some peak-baggers killed.

My backpack has a few emergency supplies, such as matches, water, compass, whistle, and multi-purpose knife, but a little bad luck—like swirling snow or pouring rain—could make a night in the woods a recipe for disaster. If I ever get into climbing in a big way, maybe I'll buy one of those space-age thermal emergency blankets that is a proven lifesaver. But the most important survival tool is the thing between your ears, particularly when you use it to ask yourself, "What is the safe course of action?" For me, just an intermediate-level climber, turning around is the right thing to do.

I start back down the trail, thinking how ridiculous it is that I was so focused on reaching the top, I overlooked enjoying the journey up. There should be no goal, just enjoyment of the outing. If you reach the top, great. If you can climb all the really big mountains, the 4,000-footers, that's great too, if you enjoy the process, the journey, the thrill of discovery. But if you try to "collect" a mountain, notch it in your belt, you miss the very essence of the experience. Mountains bring a spiritual renewal, and the physical act of climbing is the therapy, the cleansing of the soul for the summit. But the *whole* mountain is a sacred place, not just the summit, as I find out on the way down. Exhausted, cold and disappointed, the mountain gives me a wake-up call in the form of a crimson flash. It's the red crest of a pileated woodpecker, swooping through the trees, ringing out its odd call. In the gray forest, still under the grip of winter, the reward of the woodpecker brought a smile to me. This is why I do it, I thought, the little elemental things that go unnoticed when you're inside, surrounded by artificial light and

sound. And I'm here for the physical joy of climbing, no different than the "high" runners get.

Every sport has its highs, but mountain-climbing thrills
have to be tempered with logic, especially climbs in the cold-
weather months. Every year someone overestimates his strength,
and underestimates the weather, winding up in real trouble on a
forlorn peak. Survivors often tell a similar story, how a front
moved in so quickly they found themselves in a near-whiteout
when just an hour before there had been unlimited sunshine.
Temperatures can plunge twenty degrees, conspiring with the
wind to sap strength. The mountain and the rock are indiffer-
ent to pleas for help.

One of the most chilling stories of man and the dangers of
the forest and of winter in particular was written by Jack London in his classic story, *To Build a Fire.* In it the main character
is traveling with his dog in the Yukon on a severely cold day—
fifty degrees below zero—when calamity strikes, twice. First he
breaks through thin ice covering a spring and wets his leg, then,
when he lights a fire, the tree limb just above his flames dumps
its load of snow, extinguishing the fire. His extremities are so
frozen he is unable to move his hands and cannot light the fire
again. In a last desperate effort he leaps on his dog, with the
idea that he will kill it and warm his hands inside the dog's
body. Even though he has the dog encircled in his arms, he
cannot manipulate his hands to draw his knife or throttle the
dog, and the man dies.

London's prose is so intense, you feel the cold seeping into
your bones as you read the story. Not only do we see the terror
unfold through the eyes of the man, but London also lets us see

the events from the dog's simple perspective; no easy feat for a writer to pull off.

In the opening pages London alludes to why the man will get in trouble:

"The trouble with him was that he was without imagination. He was quick and alert in the things of life, but only in the things, and not in the significances. Fifty degrees below zero meant eighty-odd degrees of frost. Such fact impressed him as being cold and uncomfortable, and that was all. It did not lead him to meditate upon his frailty as a creature of temperature, and upon man's frailty in general, able only to live within certain narrow limits of heat and cold: and from there on it did not lead him to the conjectural field of immortality and man's place in the universe."

If ever a story serves as warning to expect the unexpected when traveling the forest alone, this one is it.

* * * *

Once at the bottom I drive south looking for something, anything, hot, to eat or drink. In West Burke I hit the brakes when I see a wooden bear standing atop an old porch. Stranger than the bear is the name of the store: Bertha's Burger Bar and General Store. Peeking inside, I decide to give it a shot. I'm served a piping hot bowl of chili, and scarf it down, surrounded by fishing tackle, clothing and hardware. Ah, the creature comforts.

More comforts follow when I check into the WillowVale Inn, on the northern end of Lake Willoughby, where I immediately soak in a hot bath. Is there a better feeling after a day outdoors in the cold?

The WilloghVale Inn, with its fine restaurant, is a magnet for both locals and travelers, where both can come together and trade stories over the cherrywood bar in the pub. During dinner I talk with an elderly gentleman named John who lives on the lake. All of us have a special place, and he describes his in a poignant way:

"I'm seventy-five now, but I remember the first time I came here on vacation when I was ten years old—I had the feeling I was home. Even when I lived in different areas of the U. S., I still considered Willoughby my home. It took me until I was almost sixty to finally settle here for good, but now I wake up and look right down the gap, all the way to Burke Mountain, just like I dreamed."

I know exactly what he meant. I had the same feeling the first time I stayed at the old Rutledge Inn on Lake Morey in Vermont, and have dreamed of living on that lake ever since. Vermont has a way of getting in your blood, of tugging at you until you come back. I went to college in Vermont, then bought my cabin at the edge of the Kingdom shortly after. My brother Mark loved the state so much he moved here for good a few years back, and someday maybe I'll do the same.

Every region of Vermont has its subtle differences, but it's the people of the Kingdom who consider themselves the true Vermonters. Fiercely independent and self-sufficient, they love the Kingdom for what it is—wild, remote and isolated. In a real sense it's a frontier, with frontier hardships. Both the economy (few jobs) and the climate (brutal seven-month winters followed by the quagmire of mud season) seem to conspire against these hill people. Yet they stay and they love it, though I doubt they would use the word "love" to describe their quiet passion for the land. And for some reason, perhaps because it offers independent thinkers the room for individuality, the Kingdom has attracted some of the country's finest writers, such as Edward Hoagland and Howard Frank Mosher.

How did this corner of Vermont get its name? It's said that George Aiken, a former senator from Vermont, was the first to refer to the counties of Orleans, Essex and Caledonia as the Northeast Kingdom. While fishing in Essex County, he was touched by the beauty surrounding him, and gazing up at the hills said, "this place should have a special name; we should call it the Northeast Kingdom." That was in the 1950s, and since then the Kingdom has shown signs of change, particularly in the number of out-of-state "flatlanders" who have bought summer homes or moved here for good. One thing I've heard over and over about newcomers is that they come here to escape the suburbs or the city, then the first thing they do is try to change the area to be like their former homes. And what really burns the true Vermonters is seeing a newcomer buy a large block of land and post it. Prime hunting grounds, used for generations by the locals, are now off limits. When I hear that scenario, all I can think of is how the native Americans must have felt when the Europeans told them that not only could they not live in such and such an area, but they couldn't hunt there either.

* * * *

The best inns usually have a topnotch library of regional books, and the WillowVale is no exception. The books on Lake Willoughby keep me up much later than I intend, but when you read about other's experiences in the very place you are exploring, who can think of sleep? I read that the origin of the name Mount Pisgah is biblical—a mountain in Jordan from which Moses saw the Promised Land—and Mount Hor was named for the place where Mose's brother Aaron died and was buried. Another book says that Abraham climbed Pisgah, but was stopped fifty feet from the summit! Maybe it was the curse of Abraham that forced me off the mountain.

The lake, I learn, is almost five miles long, less than a mile wide, and said to be 308 feet deep. Such depths make it a first-class cold-water fishery, with landlocked salmon, some monster browns, and lake trout that usually take the state's annual record. In fact, Vermont's current record lake trout, a thirty-four pounder, was pulled from Willoughby. And like all deep lakes, this one has its monster sightings. In 1986 a woman from New Jersey saw a large aquatic creature, and fifteen years earlier a two-humped creature was sighted. Even as far back as 1868 *The Caledonian* reported that a boy killed a great snake in the lake: "Rushing boldly upon the monster he severed the body with a sickle. The two pieces were found to be 23 feet."

Surprisingly, instead of draining south like most New England waterways, the lake drains north into Lake Memphremagog, then continues to Canada and the St. Lawrence. In the mid nineteenth century, Willoughby was a popular resort referred to as the "Lucerne of America." The Lake House at the southern end and Giman's Tavern at Westmore Village housed guests from across the country, while steamboats carried them on tours. The lake inspired visitors in the twentieth century as

well, as evidenced in a poem written in 1911 by Eva Margaret
Smith, simply called *Lake Willoughby:*

> Watched over by vast sentinels of rock
> Surrounded by the gloom of forests deep
> Thy waves leap high in boisterous playfulness
> Or peaceful calm in sleep.

> The sunset glory falls on Pisgah's height,
> Clothing that rugged form with beauty rare,
> While numerous waves lap gently on the shore,
> A lullaby to care.

> O beauteous lake and forest-laden hills
> Where shadow fall and endless breezes blow
> Almost thou seemest in our troubled age
> An Eden here below.

* * * *

There are countless gravel back roads to explore in the Kingdom, and I spend the next day wandering the countryside to
the northwest of Willoughby, passing through Brownington
and Barton. Brownington is known to history lovers because of
The Old Stone House Museum, which bills itself as "the rarest
kind of museum: a building as fascinating as the collection it
houses." Made of granite blocks, and looking like a fortress, it
was designed and erected in the 1830s by a man believed to be
America's first black college graduate and first black legislator,
the Reverend Alexander Twilight. Twilight was on a mission:
he quarried the stone, dressed the blocks, and dragged them to
the site with a single ox, where he spent three years of his life
constructing his stone house. Although the thirty-room monu-
ment looks like a garrison, Twilight used it as a school where he
taught the region's children.

The Twilight story is one of courage and individuality, and I especially like it because it's so different than the Irasburg Affair of 1968, where racial prejudice forced a black family to leave the little town of Irasburg. It's a sad story, and was used as the inspiration for Howard Frank Mosher's dark novel, *A Stranger In The Kingdom.* Every region has its good people and bad, and the Kingdom is no exception.

Near The Old Stone House is Prospect Hill, just up the road a bit, next to a tiny church in Brownington. I walk to the top of the hill and to the observation platform, and drink in the scene. Two layers of cloud cover are floating over the valley, one far overhead blocking out the sun, and another narrow band at treetop level. Between these stratums, mile after endless mile of mountains stretch to the horizons. The distinctive gap of Willoughby, framed by the twin mountains of Pisgah and Hor, dominates the southern horizon, while in the foreground the steeple of a church knifes through the low cloud cover.

I meditate on the platform, thankful to be alive in such a place of beauty. Then, as I'm leaving, I notice a dark outline in a huge old sugar maple at the corner of the field. On closer inspection I see that it's a porcupine, nipping off the buds of the tree. I should be content to take my picture and leave, but instead I climb the tree, first up the trunk then inching out on the branch, hoping for the perfect photograph. But wildlife never cooperates. I figure the porcupine will climb farther out on the branch, but instead it makes a U-turn and begins its descent—with me directly in its path. For a brief moment I'm face-to-face with this beady-eyed creature, separated by about five feet, with the gap narrowing as it keeps coming.

Porcupines can't throw their quills, but this one won't need to in another second, and I almost fall out of the maple, sliding backwards, scraping my hands, doing an awkward shimmy back down. Serves me right.

Porcupines hold a fascination for me, probably dating back to my boyhood when two of them scared the life out of me. My family was staying at a remote cabin in the Berkshires, and my brother and I slept on the porch. Some time in the middle of one night, blood-curdling screams and screeches—no more than a few feet away—woke us in terror. The screams were high-pitched and maniacal. When they subsided, we mustered the courage to venture outside with our flashlights, scanning the ground. We could see nothing and turned to go back in the porch when a shrill cry pierced our ears, coming not from the woods but from directly overhead in an old apple tree. With shaking hands, we shone our flashlights on the culprits—two porcupines. Maybe they were fighting, or maybe they were making love, but whatever it was we both never forgot those screams. Only the wailing bark of a fox floating through a dark night is as scary.

Porcupines will den anywhere it's dry, favoring granite ledges, but also using old culverts and even outhouses! (I had one appear in my outhouse, and yes, there was a close call of the posterior kind.) It's a lackadaisical animal, feeling secure in all its thirty thousand quills, and it usually moves slowly. But when threatened it can whip its tail around with surprising speed, and more than one dog has got a nose full of quills. When a porcupine quill enters the body it absorbs moisture and expands, working deeper, even as much as an inch a day. If it hits a vital organ, it's lights out. But in spite of its armor, there are a few predators, like the mountain lion and fisher, who can kill porcupines. The fisher does so by circling the porcupine, nipping at its exposed face and tiring it through a long dance of loss of blood and death.

After the porcupine incident I ramble over to the village of Orleans in Barton to watch the rainbows run the Willoughby River. Each spring the fish leave Lake Memphremagog to spawn in the Willoughby. There is a small waterfall here, and after waiting and watching for twenty minutes I see a five-pounder leap the falls in a silver blur. Anglers line the banks below the falls, primarily fishing with spawn sacks and bait in hopes of dueling with these Memphremagog rainbows. My rod is in the car, but with twenty anglers already scattered along the river it doesn't look like my cup of tea.

The best part of trout fishing for me is the "hunting" aspect, walking carefully up the river, searching out productive pockets and trying for the perfect presentation. It calls for stealth and full attention, whereby you become absorbed in the pursuit, and time seems suspended. Hours can go by or just minutes, but either way you forget about every other aspect of your life—and that's the beauty of it. If I'm in one spot for long, whether it's in a boat or on shore, the thrill just isn't there.

So I head southwestward to the Lamoille River, an old favorite. It's a good-sized river, rising in the Kingdom in the village of Greensboro and flowing westward, out of the Kingdom, covering eighty-five miles before reaching Lake Champlain. Its headwaters hold brook trout and rainbows, with good growth

rates due to dissolved minerals, such as magnesium and calcium, that naturally leach into the water from the soil and
rocks. Over the years I've fished the river probably close to a
hundred times, with good success on most occasions. And it
will take another hundred times to explore sections of the river
I've yet to walk.

Just about the entire run of the Lamoille holds trout. The
stretch along Route 16, where the river runs shallow and swift,
has small trout in the riffles and pools. Even in Hardwick center, trout hold behind rocks in the rapids near the Village Café,
and farther west in Wolcott, where train whistles crack the silence as they rumble through the covered railroad bridge, trout
hide beneath undercut banks. In Morrisville and Johnson the
river broadens, and holes up to thirty feet deep hold brown
trout of legendary proportions. Between Jeffersonville and
Fairfax trout somehow survive in the relatively warm water,
mixed with bass and other warm-water species. Even the mouth
of the Lamoille gave me the gift of good fishing, not of trout,
but of a northern pike, three feet long, battling for more than
half an hour.

The tributaries are productive as well—the Wild Branch,
Green River, Gihon River, North Branch and the Brewster
River. Just saying their names bring back memories of the people I fished with and even the trout themselves. Fish may not
have a personality, but given enough time to reflect on a
memorable day of fishing, I usually think of a particular fish
caught or lost on that outing. And over time the trout becomes
not just a fish, but an individual creature blending in with the
whole experience. The friend I fish with, the river, and the

trout become an important memory, and memories are really as much of who we are as any other facet of the mind.

The particular fish I remember best was not the largest, nor the best battler, but a rainbow I caught in the upper reaches of the river. It was a day when the fishing was so slow, I was casting more for the fun of casting than actually to catch a fish. Memory has a way of tricking the mind into thinking you hooked the fish on the last cast, but that's how I remember it. I had put on a heavy, gold-colored lure, hoping it would change my luck, but after another fishless hour I decided the last cast would simply be done to see how far I could chuck the thing. My lure shot forward like it came out of sling shot, sailing way upstream, where it splashed down alongside a boulder in the middle of the river. An instant later a fish cleared the water a full two feet. It took a second for me to realize it was on the end of my line. The next few minutes turned the whole day around. It was a rainbow trout, strong as can be, and it leapt time and time again before I finally netted it. I can still see that first jump in the distance like it happened yesterday.

Now, as I walk the river, I'm using a fly rod, casting sinking tip line with a brass-head woolly bugger attached; anything to get the offering deep. The water is running high and fast, with more of a brown hue than blue. If the trout are active, they are not showing themselves, and chances are that most are in the deepest holes, where they can conserve energy away from the current. Still, I cast repeatedly to boulders in the middle of the stream, hoping a rainbow will catapult from the depths into my world of air and light. But if the fish are there, they aren't budging. I change tacks, and walk the river, not stopping till

I'm at the one of the deepest holes I know of just north of Wolcott. Here I dredge the bottom, using the fly rod the same way
a kid would drift a worm. There's a tap on my line, I set the
hook, and feel quivering life on the other end. The fish goes
upstream, then tears down, keeping away from the surface. I'm
able to turn it, and now it feels like dead weight in the current.
Lifting my rod, the fish comes up, thrashing on the surface, but
not leaping. It's a brown, about twelve inches. Guiding it into
my net, I see the fight has left the fish, having spent itself on
both the line and current. It's the first fish of the year. Sprinkled with salt and pan fried, it would make a great meal. But
being the first fish of the year, it wins a reprieve and I watch it
sink, then glide upstream and head back where it came from.

Now that I know where the fish are, know the weighted
woolly bugger is what they want, I expect to catch more, and
work my way from hole to hole, sometimes walking, sometimes
driving. I go all the way to where the Green River spills into the
Lamoille. It's a unique tributary, with water temperatures fairly
constant in all seasons because it originates at the
impoundment of the Green Reservoir. In the summer the
Green River carries colder water to the Lamoille, and in the
spring it's actually a bit warmer than the river below. I figure
maybe the trout will be more active and less sluggish below this
confluence, but nothing stirs. Although these early spring days
of high, discolored water offer an angler the best chance of
fooling a truly big brown, nothing takes my offerings.

That night I go to my cabin and eat sardines from a can.
It's a clear night, with a million stars reflecting pinpoints of
light from the heavens. I sleep out on the porch, listening to the

hoots of owls and thinking of other nights on porches long ago, wondering if there are any porcupines nearby.

* * * *

At dawn I drive to Victory Bog. It's a unique natural area, covering roughly 20,000 acres in a valley which has the second largest tract of boreal forest in Vermont. Within this basin are 1,800 acres of wetlands between the villages of North Concord and the Gallup Mills section of Granby. Curling through the valley is the Moose River and Bog Brook.

Wildlife abounds—moose, bear, coyote, beaver, fox, mink, fisher, otter, muskrat, bobcat—if it lives in Vermont, chances are it lives here. But the real draw for a nature lover is the abundant bird life in the diverse habitat of marsh, bog, spruce forest, red maple swamps and rivers carving through hardwoods. Great blue heron, bitterns, and green heron stalk the marsh, while osprey and kingfishers perch on dead tree limbs scanning the water for fish. Red-tailed hawks circle above, and marsh hawks hover over meadows looking for mice and voles. Smaller birds such as swamp swallows, spotted sandpipers, and redwing blackbirds are commonly seen, along with a wide variety of ducks. Great horned owls make nocturnal forays into the marsh, looking to swoop down on rabbits and skunks. And more than one motorist, driving through the fog-filled bog at night, has caught the long shape of what appeared to be a mountain lion in his headlights.

The plant life is as diverse as the wildlife. Indian cucumber, leatherleaf, sheep laurel and countless other plants, including the carnivorous sundew and pitcher plant, thrive deep in the interior in a twenty-five acre scrub-shrub boreal bog. Tamarack and spruce climb up the hills, while alders and meadowsweet crowd along the channel of the Moose River.

From North Concord a forlorn stretch of gravel road runs through the heart of the Victory Bog, following the Moose River upstream, past the frontier village of Victory and into the Victory Bog Wildlife Management Area. Victory has a population of about thirty, but at one time it had a dozen operating sawmills and its own railroad spur. I drive this road, through dark forests that give way to wetlands where a grassy marsh stretches far in all directions until encircled by rising mountains. The road, set up on a raised bed of gravel, allows one to cruise through marsh that normally would be seen only from a canoe.

Two young moose are lying down in a sedge meadow, and rise to their feet as my car inches closer. I kill the engine and roll down the window. They rise, turn their backs on me, and trot off, their hooves making a sucking sound in the muck.

Now I'm outside of the car, and the silence hits me. But it's not the desolate, lonely silence I felt a couple days earlier on Mount Pisgah, but rather the silence of a sleeping beast. There are signs of spring in the greenery, and ducks are winging their way back and forth over the marsh. The scent of dank, rich earth fills the air. It feels as though the marsh is ready to explode from its winter slumber, a life force ready to spring from the primordial ooze.

I try to walk along the river, but the ground is too soft and the trees and shrub too tangled to get far. Instead, not far from the road, I find little pockets of dry land from which to fish near the water's edge. I only fish for a short time, then go back to the car, where I look over the atlas, noting that there are barely any roads east of Victory Bog, all the way to the Connecticut River.

It's 9:00 a.m. now, and I think of a big breakfast in St. Johnsbury. A car comes by and the driver asks if I'm lost. I tell him I'm just exploring, looking for wildlife.

"Well," he says, "about a quarter mile down the road I just saw a big bull moose; it's probably still there."

That's all I need to hear. Breakfast is forgotten. I shoulder my pack, attach the zoom lens to my camera, and follow the road deeper into Victory Bog.

EXPLORER'S NOTES
Recommended reading

Northern Borders, by Howard Frank Mosher, is a poignant novel about growing up in the Northeast Kingdom.

Walking The Dead Diamond River, by Edward Hoagland, is a New England classic for those who love the wilderness and straight talk.

Victory Bog

The Vermont Department of Fisheries and Wildlife in St. Johnsbury offers rough trail maps and additional information. Trails lead into Victory Bog Wildlife Management Area from a parking area called Mitchell's Landing in Victory. The small parking area is located about four and half miles up the side road to Victory from U.S. Highway 2. The Moose River Trail is two tenths of a mile south of the parking area on the entrance road.

Mount Pisgah area

Mount Pisgah (USGS 7.5' Sutton Provisional) and Mount Hor (USGS 7.5' Sutton) are both located in Willoughby State Forest, spanning 7,300 acres. The *Vermont Atlas and Gazetteer,* published by Delorme, is very helpful when planning a hike or back-road ramble. *Fifty Hikes in Vermont,* published by Back-country Press, has trail maps to Mount Pisgah and Mount Hor.

The trail head for Mount Pisgah can be found about half a mile south of Lake Willoughby at a parking lot on Route 5A (the Mount Hor parking area is about 1.8 miles up a dirt road that leads west from the Mount Pisgah parking area.) Some people prefer to get to Mount Pisgah from a logging road access off Mill Brook Road, off Route 5A about 1.5 miles south of the junction of Route 5A and Route 16 at the north end of the lake. There is also a South Shore Trail along the lake that begins at a small parking area near the beach at the south end of the lake.

Accommodations

The WilloughVale Inn (1-800-541-0588) offers luxury befitting a Kingdom, with handcrafted furniture, fine dining, a library, veranda, and nine charming guest rooms. The inn also rents lakeside cottages.

White Caps Campground (802-467-3345).

Old Stone House Museum (802-754-2022).

Northeast Kingdom Chamber of Commerce (800-639-6379).

Northeast Kingdom Tours by bus, (802-334-TOUR).

About the Author

Michael Tougias is the author of several books about New England:

Until I Have No Country: A Novel of King Philip's Indian War
Autumn Trails
Quiet Places of Massachusetts
Nature Walks in Eastern Massachusetts
Nature Walks in Central and Western Massachusetts
Country Roads of Massachusetts
Exploring the Hidden Charles
A Taunton River Journey

Mr. Tougias gives narrated slide presentations for each of his books, including *New England Wild Places*. If you are interested in his slide presentations or his publications, please write to him at P.O. Box 72, Norfolk, MA 02056.